REAL KIDS
REAL ADVENTURES

NUMBER 1

REAL KIDS
REAL ADVENTURES
TRUE STORIES BY DEBORAH MORRIS

NUMBER 1

FIRESTORM!

PLANE CRASH ON CHRISTMAS DAY

LOST IN HIDDEN TREASURE MINE

BROADMAN
& HOLMAN
PUBLISHERS

Nashville, Tennessee

© 1994
Broadman & Holman Publishers

Printed in the United States of America

4240-51
0-8054-4051-8

Dewey Decimal Classification: JSC
Subject Heading: Courage—Nonfiction // Faith—Nonfiction
Library of Congress Card Catalog Number: 94-11741

Library of Congress Cataloging-in-Publication Data
Morris, Deborah, 1956–

Real kids, real adventures / by Deborah Morris.

p.   cm.

ISBN 0-8054-4051-8

1. Christian biography—United States—Juvenile literature.
2. Children—United States—Biography—Juvenile literature.
[1. Survival. 2. Adventure and adventurers.   3. Christian
biography.]   I. Title.
BR1714.M67   1994
209'.2'273—dc20   94-11741
[B]   CIP
                                                                  AC

To kids everywhere
who secretly imagine themselves facing great danger
with courage, strength, and heroism.

Firestorm!

The Kathleen and Keith Hedges Story

"Keith! Do you think this'll stay on?" Kathleen Hedges, sixteen, was twisting around trying to see the garbage bag full of popcorn she'd tied to her backpack. Keith, her fifteen-year-old brother, laughed. "It looks dumb, but I guess it'll stay. Come on, we need to get started. Dad will be waiting for us."

It was about ten o'clock on Saturday morning, August 20, 1988; the two teenagers were standing on a hilltop above their family's "base camp" in Montana's Absaroka-

1

Beartooth Wilderness. Their younger sister and brother, Angie and Jens, and twenty-one-year-old foster brother, Walter American Horse, were waiting with their mother to wave good-bye. The teenagers were supposed to cut across the wilderness to meet their father that afternoon near Horseshoe Creek, about eight miles away.

"Be careful!" Mrs. Hedges reminded them, as usual. Keith flashed her an impish grin. "Oh, gee, Mom, do we have to?" She laughed. The brother and sister started down the steep, wooded slope, noting the faint smoky smell in the mountain air. For the last few months, fires had been smoldering across nearby Yellowstone National Park.

Kathleen smiled, flipping her shoulder-length blond hair out of her face. "This is going to be fun. And Dad will really be surprised when he sees all this popcorn. This should be enough for us to snack on all week!"

"More like all *month*," Keith said. "You look like Santa Claus with that garbage bag. Ho-ho-ho!" Kathleen just rolled her eyes.

Despite the long hike in front of them, they were both in a buoyant mood. The idea of forging alone through the wilderness was exciting. After meeting their father, they planned to spend the next week hiking and fishing with him before returning to camp.

They fell into an easy walking rhythm as they crunched down the slope side by side. "So," Keith said, "are you still gonna move out to California when you graduate?"

"Probably. Either there or maybe Florida. Someplace warm, anyway, with water." Kathleen paused to shove her way past some thorny bushes. "Ow!" she yelped. "What are these things?"

"I don't know, but they just tore a big hole in your bag. Popcorn's spilling everywhere."

Kathleen looked back. "Oh, no! Can you tie a little knot in it or something?"

"I guess." He moved behind her and started fiddling with the plastic bag.

As she waited, Kathleen gazed at the next mountain peak. "You know, I had imagined nice rolling hills, but it's steep! And thorny." She rubbed her arm ruefully. "At least it's not raining. But doesn't the sun look weird?"

The recent wildfires had left the sky smudged with gray haze, turning the sun a bright, angry red. Keith finished repairing the popcorn bag and squinted upward. "Yeah . . . looks like a great big cherry."

They started off again, and before long were talking enthusiastically about their favorite topic—getting rich.

"I don't think it'd be too hard to figure out the stock market," Keith said. "Those guys are the ones who're pulling in the really big bucks."

Kathleen laughed. "You'd probably get bored after about a week. Besides, I thought you wanted to be a professional wrestler or a motorcycle racer or something."

"Yeah, well, I don't know. All I know is I want to be filthy, stinking rich. Maybe buy an island somewhere. A private one, like you see on TV."

"Sounds good. A tropical island with lots of banana trees and pineapples." Kathleen smiled dreamily. "We could build a big castle and have our own limo. And we could have a bunch of exotic animals—monkeys and zebras and llamas—"

"Yeah, and we'd only invite special friends that we really wanted to see," Keith added firmly.

Their plans for the future were interrupted when Kathleen glanced back to discover she was leaving a trail of popcorn again. She made an exasperated sound and stopped. "My bag's sprung another leak," she said. "Keith, can you—?"

Her brother sighed. "You're worse than Hansel, or was it Gretel? You know, the kid who left a trail of bread crumbs. By the time we get to Dad it'll all be gone, and there'll be a bunch of fat squirrels waddling around the woods."

"Yeah, right. Just fix the bag, will you?"

"Yes, master. Whatever you say, master." He ducked, grinning, when Kathleen swung around to pop him on the forehead.

Popcorn once again secure, they continued down the trail, talking companionably. From the time they were very small they'd done almost everything together: made up their own games to play, defended each other when they were in trouble, encouraged each other when they were down. It wasn't surprising that whenever they talked about the future they included each other in their plans.

They walked almost two hours before reaching a small stream. As they followed it, Kathleen suddenly caught a glimpse of something through the trees.

"Hey, look over there!" she said. "A man on a horse!"

As they got closer they saw that it was an older man wearing a battered, brown cowboy hat. He was leading two pack horses. They nodded as he passed.

"He must be a prospector," Kathleen murmured, spotting the worn gold pan lashed onto one of his packs. "I guess he's out here checking the streams." She smiled suddenly. "Remember the camping trip where Dad showed us how to pan for gold?"

"Uh-huh. We were so excited when we found those microscopic gold specks! We could've made a fortune at it if we'd had, say, two or three hundred years."

Kathleen giggled. "Yeah. Kind of like your get-rich-quick plan when you built that airplane out of Dad's old plywood. You were going to make a fortune charging your friends for rides."

Keith nodded. "I'm just glad Dad caught us before we pushed it off the edge of the riverbank. Thirty feet straight down, and splat!"

They stopped for lunch at around one o'clock, both glad to slip out of their heavy backpacks and sink down onto the springy cushion of pine needles.

Kathleen leaned back against a tree, rubbing her aching shoulders. "How much farther do you think it'll be to the bridge? Dad said it would only take three or four hours, but you know how he is."

Keith rooted around in his pack to pull out a map. "It looks like we're just about here," he pointed to a spot on the topographic map, which showed high and low spots like mountains and canyons, "and if so, we're not even quite halfway yet."

"I should've known," Kathleen sighed.

Their father, a red-haired fire captain, had a bad habit of always thinking things would take less time than they did. It was a standing joke in the family. But now, as tired as they were, it wasn't all that funny. In another three or four hours it would be dark!

The siblings fixed a quick lunch of Spam™ sandwiches and then slipped into their backpacks again. The packs seemed, if possible, even heavier than before. Why had they carried so much junk?

"My feet hurt," Kathleen eventually complained. "I think I'm getting some blisters."

"Yeah, me too," said Keith. "Hey, why don't we trade tennis shoes? That way they won't be rubbing the same spots."

"Okay," Kathleen replied.

They stopped and exchanged shoes and then started off again, both of them happier. Good thing they wore the same size!

An hour later, climbing a steep stretch of the trail, Keith noticed an interesting recess in the rocks above them. "Hang on a minute," he said.

Scrambling up the hillside, he discovered a small cave. He glanced around the entrance, and then stopped as he noticed something near the corner. There was a dark green flashlight lying abandoned on the floor. He picked it up, shook it, and clicked it on. It worked!

"Kathleen!" he shouted. "I found a flashlight up here!" He quickly clambered back down to where his sister waited. He turned the light off and on several times. "See? I think it's an Army flashlight, the kind they use at night. The lens is red."

"We might be using it at night if we don't hurry up. Let's go."

It was late that afternoon before they reached the small bridge where their father was supposed to meet them. There was no sign of him. "Dad?" Keith called, cupping his hands around his mouth.

"Dad! Are you here?"

The only sound was the running water of the small stream. Kathleen shook her head. "The way he was coming was a lot rougher," she said, pointing off toward some craggy peaks. "He'll probably be here in a few minutes."

Setting her pack on the end of the bridge, she opened it and dug around until she found a bag of pistachios. "Here, you want some?" Keith nodded, and she shook some out into his cupped palm. They sat on the bridge side by side, munching pistachios and tossing the pink shells into the running stream.

"I wonder how Misty's liking all this," Kathleen said. Misty was their family dog, an excitable black and tan mutt they'd raised from a puppy. Their dad had taken her along for company when he'd hiked off into the wilderness several days earlier.

"She's having a blast," Keith said. "Probably terrorizing all the squirrels. Especially all the *fat* squirrels that chowed down on your popcorn!"

Kathleen laughed. "Remember how she used to play with the mice out in the barn? She kind of juggled with them, caught them by their tails, and tossed them up in the air over and over again."

Keith snapped his fingers. "Maybe that's how we can get rich!" he said with exaggerated excitement. "We'll start a television show: 'The Amazing Misty, World-Famous Canine Mouse-Juggler!'"

"Uh-huh. That's *almost* as good as your great idea for self-lighting cigarettes. If people didn't blow their faces off first, they could live long enough to die of cancer." She suddenly grinned. "The pistachios rubbed off all over your mouth. You look like you're wearing bright pink lipstick."

"So? There's nobody here to see me." He cracked another nut between his teeth and peeled off the shells. "I just wish Dad would get here."

"Why don't we hide down under the bridge and scare him when he comes? He deserves it after making us sit here all this time."

"Okay."

Grabbing their backpacks, they scrambled down the bank and settled into a dry, cozy spot just out of sight beneath the end of the wooden bridge.

Ten minutes later, their father walked up. "Kathleen? Keith?"

They held their breath, smiling, but they'd forgotten about Misty. She galloped straight over to their hiding place and greeted them joyfully, jumping and licking their faces.

"Misty, you ruined it!" Kathleen said, fending her off. Keith crawled out from under the bridge and stood up.

"Hi, Dad. What took you so long?"

Mr. Hedges came over to join them. "This is pretty rough country. I had to make my own trail most of the way. It took longer than I expected."

"No joke," Keith said, giving Kathleen a humorous look. "We had a trail, but it was still a long way. We ran into a gold miner with some horses. Oh, and I found a flashlight somebody left up in a cave!"

"You should've left it. They might come back for it."

"No way! I bet it'd been laying there for days."

Since it was late, they decided to start looking right away for a place to camp. A flat place with no rocks, close to water, would be ideal.

"Let's head up Horseshoe Creek," Mr. Hedges suggested. "There should be someplace once we get higher."

It took almost two more hours to find a spot. They hiked down into a densely wooded box canyon and then back up the other side. They finally stopped at a small clearing overlooking the gorge.

They jumped into action to set up camp, knowing it would be much harder once it was dark. Pulling large sheets of plastic from their packs, they spread them out on the ground and then laid their sleeping bags out on top. The groundsheets would keep the dampness away from them as they slept.

Then they dug a fire pit and lined it with flat rocks. Soon Mr. Hedges had a cheerful blaze going.

"Canned chili sound okay?" he asked.

"Sounds great," Keith answered. "We're starving."

Thirty minutes later they were hunched over steaming bowls of chili, sipping sugarless Kool-aid™ from tin cups. Afterward they snacked on popcorn and then finished the meal off with foamy cups of hot chocolate.

"Now I know what those poor squirrels feel like," Keith groaned, leaning back to pat his stomach. "I don't think I ever want to see popcorn again."

They rinsed the dishes and gratefully crawled into their down-filled sleeping bags. Misty laid down beside Kathleen and put her cold nose next to Kathleen's ear with a sleepy sigh. Although the dog belonged to the whole family, she was especially close to Kathleen. By morning she would probably have wormed her way all the way down inside the sleeping bag.

Kathleen stroked Misty as she gazed up thoughtfully at the night sky. She had always enjoyed sleeping outside, but tonight the smoky haze had blotted out the stars overhead. Even the moon was barely visible. The only light was an eerie reddish glow showing over the three jagged peaks behind them, reflecting in the low-hanging clouds above.

"Is that from the fires over at Yellowstone?" she asked her father. "It looks kind of pretty."

"Probably from the Storm Creek fire," he replied. "They've got two guys monitoring it around the clock. It's pretty far away, though."

"That's good." Kathleen fell silent, still watching the red clouds. For some reason she felt restless tonight. She snuggled Misty closer, wondering idly if there were any grizzlies prowling around. If so, the dog would be a good early-warning system.

It took her a few minutes to notice that the red clouds were rapidly expanding across the night sky. Frowning, she twisted her body around in her sleeping bag to glance back at the three peaks she'd looked at earlier. Was it her imagination, or was the glow getting brighter?

Flames in the Distance!

Kathleen settled back uneasily, noting that the eerie red clouds had now spread all the way across the sky to the canyon at her feet. But it wasn't until she saw a distinct flickering movement reflected in the sky over the canyon that she sat up in alarm.

She stared in disbelief. *Flames were shooting up over the opposite canyon wall!* "Dad!" she said, struggling out of her sleeping bag.

"Dad! I think the fire's coming!"

Mr. Hedges sat up, blinking sleepily. His eyes widened as he followed her gaze to see a wall of flames over a hundred feet high shooting up above the ridge. He scrambled to his feet.

"Wake Keith up. We've got to get out of here!"

Kathleen obeyed without question. Running over to her brother, she knelt beside him and started shaking his shoulder. "Keith, get up!" she said. *"Now!"*

He finally opened his eyes. "What?" he asked irritably.

Kathleen shook him again, harder. "Fire!" she said. "Come on!"

Keith lifted his head to look. His jaw instantly dropped. An ocean of flames was now spilling down the ridge opposite them, swallowing everything in its path as it roared down into the canyon like some kind of hellish flood. Tall pine trees flared, sending hungry flames licking upward like torches. The roar of the wind sounded like a distant freight train.

Keith froze, mesmerized by the incredible sight. It was like something out of Dante's *Inferno* or a very bad nightmare!

Mr. Hedges jolted him out of his reverie. "Come on! Grab your shoes and sleeping bag. We've got to get to the creek!"

"The creek?" Keith had already leaped to his feet. "No way. We should head up to the lake!"

"Don't argue with me!" Mr. Hedges snapped. "We'd never make it to the lake in time. It's all straight uphill."

"But—"

"No buts! I know what I'm talking about. This isn't a normal fire—it's a firestorm! It can move as fast as a tornado. The creek is nearer, and that's where we're going!"

Keith stared at his father, before nodding. Misty whined, and Kathleen ran over to grab her. When they left camp a moment later it was to head, against all instincts, directly toward the fire.

The night air was thick with smoke as they plunged into the tangled underbrush and started fighting their way toward the creek. Sharp branches clawed at their faces and clothes as they shouted repeatedly to each other, afraid they'd get separated in the swirling haze. The wind had become a thundering roar.

Although the main blaze was still several miles away, flames spread by the wind were starting to leap from treetop to treetop overhead, sending sparks and burning branches plummeting to earth all around them. Spot fires were erupting on every side, flaring up like small torches.

Deer must feel like this when they're trapped in a forest fire, Kathleen thought, her heart pounding. She stepped over a burning branch, shuddering as she imagined what it would be like if the fire overtook them. Would their flesh actually *melt?*

Then she heard her father's voice, a faint shout almost carried away by the wind. "I see the creek!"

Kathleen stared in dismay when she saw the water. It was barely eight inches deep, and even that was thickly studded with dry boulders. As Keith ran up, she saw the same disbelief reflected in his face.

He looked over at her, raising one dark eyebrow. "Well, I'll see you in heaven!"

His words angered her. "Shut up! That doesn't help."

The rising wind felt like a blast furnace. They all whirled in alarm when a burning pine tree behind them toppled with a sharp *crack!* and spewed flaming branches and pine needles in every direction. Kathleen shrieked as a burning pine needle hit her cheek.

Mr. Hedges glanced around, spotting a huge log lying across the creek just downstream. If they got back under it, they'd have at least some protection.

"Come on!" he shouted as another tree thundered to the ground nearby, spraying sparks into the dry underbrush. Kathleen and Keith hurried after him. He led them down to the water's edge near the log but hesitated, squinting through the smoke to gauge the fire's distance.

"Listen," he said. "The fire will probably reach us in less than twenty minutes. When it does I want you to get down into the water. No matter how cold or uncomfortable you get, don't stand up! Temperatures in firestorms like this can shoot up to over a thousand degrees, hot enough to char your flesh in seconds. I want you to keep your sleeping bags soaked down and pulled all the way over you. Understand?"

"Yes, sir," Kathleen and Keith replied, their eyes wide with fear.

He continued, "I'm going back now for our packs. If we make it through all this, we're going to need our emergency supplies."

Kathleen was horrified. "You can't! You'll never make it back in time!"

"I'll make it. Just stay here, and remember what I said."

"Dad, wait!" Kathleen cried, but her anguished protest was swept away by the hot wind. On the verge of tears, she sank down and wrapped her arms around Misty, burying her face in her fur. Why did this have to happen?

"He'll be okay," Keith said as they watched their father disappear into the smoky haze. "He knows what he's doing."

The firestorm edged closer, sending a steady shower of ashes raining down around them. The main fire was now clearly visible, barely half a mile away. The air, bright as daylight, was tinted an eerie flickering red, the wind whipped into a screaming, feverish gale. Sparks fell on the grass and brush along the creek, igniting them.

Suddenly, a solid figure emerged from the thick, swirling smoke. It was their father! His face was smudged with black, but he was unhurt. He was carrying all three backpacks.

"Put these on those boulders in the water!" he said.

Kathleen and Keith quickly grabbed the packs and splashed out into the shallow creek. The water, fed from melting snow, was shockingly cold as it seeped into their shoes and lapped over their ankles. They dropped the packs onto some rocks and hurried back to dry land.

Then they watched in fascination as the fire relentlessly bore down on them. Trees in its path exploded like dynamite; the wind rose to a deafening roar that seemed to shake the ground. Finally, the air became so thick with smoke that it was hard to breathe.

"Time to get into the creek!" Mr. Hedges said, raising his voice to carry over the sound of the wind. "Bring your sleeping bags."

Misty cowered on the bank, whining, as they splashed out into the water again. It was so cold it took their breath away—especially after the hot, dry wind.

Standing ankle-deep in the water, Mr. Hedges looked at them, his face grim. "Before the fire gets here, I'd like to take a minute and pray. We're going to need some help on this one."

His matter-of-fact words shook the teenagers. Their father had always been able to handle anything that came their way—especially anything to do with the outdoors. If he needed help, things were serious.

Kathleen reached out to take Keith's hand and then her father's. They bowed their heads.

"Lord," Mr. Hedges said, "we're Your children, and You've promised to protect us in times of need. If there ever was a time we needed You, it's now! Please be with us, in Jesus' name."

"Amen," Keith said. Kathleen just squeezed his hand.

Misty was still pacing the creekbank, and she wouldn't come when Kathleen called. Kathleen finally had to drag her into the water.

"It's going to be okay," she said, cradling the trembling dog in her arms. Holding her tightly, Kathleen sat down in the stream and scooted back under the log, trying to ignore the numbing cold. Beside her, her father and Keith were also getting in position, flattening themselves in the water and pulling their wet sleeping bags up over them. The creek was so shallow that most of their bodies would be exposed.

Kathleen momentarily released her hold on Misty to tug on her own sleeping bag, but in that instant, the panicked animal wriggled free. "Misty, no!" Kathleen screamed as the dog clawed her way toward the creekbank. Once there, Misty looked around in confusion and then darted away—straight toward the approaching fire!

"Misty!" Kathleen jumped up to go after her, but her father pulled her back down.

"Let her go!" he shouted. "Better her than us! Get down and cover up!"

Kathleen obeyed. Through the din she heard Misty yelp once in pain—then abruptly fall silent. Huddling miserably in the icy water, Kathleen was unable to control her hysterical sobs. *Misty!*

"We don't have time for that now!" her father said sharply. "Save it for later."

She took a deep breath. He was right. She could cry later. Right now she had to concentrate on staying alive.

The fire was almost upon them when they heard Misty yelp again—this time much closer. "She's alive!" Kathleen gasped. "Misty, *come!*"

Mr. Hedges whistled sharply, the sound piercing even the wind's mighty roar. Misty bounded back down into the stream beside them, scared but unhurt.

"I've got her!" Mr. Hedges said. Whipping off his belt, he wrapped it around the dog's body like a halter, then pulled her down beside him.

Seconds later, the firestorm swept across the creek-bed.

The air instantly became a howling maelstrom of smoke and fire. Kathleen and Keith looked up in horror to see a giant, fiery pinwheel spinning in the air just above them, throwing off red sparks that swirled and fell to the ground like falling stars. The heat was so intense that even the rocks nearby cracked in half. Everything in sight was burning.

This must be what hell looks like, Keith thought incredulously, his teeth chattering from the numbing cold of the water. *It's like the whole world is on fire.* He had always been a thrill-seeker, the one who liked to bend the rules. But now his thoughts ran wild. *Maybe,* he thought desperately, *if I promise to be a better person in the future, God will spare us. Or at least Kathleen. She doesn't deserve to die like this.*

Inches away, her face buried in the icy water, Kathleen was thinking her own despairing thoughts. The fire was so big, and the creek so shallow.

Surely there was no way they could survive.

She pictured her mother's agony when she learned of their deaths. *Mom!* she cried silently. *I'm so sorry.*

* * *

Eight miles away, Mrs. Hedges sat up abruptly in bed. She was awakened by a voice calling urgently, "Mom!"

She jumped up and went to the camper's window to check on the kids. Angie, Jens, and Walter were all resting peacefully in their sleeping bags.

She went back to bed, puzzled and a little uneasy. It must have been a dream, she supposed. But the voice had seemed so real.

Survival by Fire

The firestorm continued to rage, devouring everything that could burn. Mr. Hedges used a kettle he'd brought from camp to splash water onto Kathleen and Keith's sleeping bags. Kathleen glanced up to see that the end of the log above her was starting to burn.

"Dad!" she shouted. "Let me use the kettle!" She scooped water and, after a few tries, put the fire out.

The blistering assault seemed to go on for an eternity. When they finally noticed that the wind was dying down, they wondered if they were imagining it. They cautiously raised their heads to look around.

The wall of fire had passed over them. It was now moving up the mountain above them.

Mr. Hedges stood up, a grin splitting his soot-blackened face. "We did it!" he yelled.

Kathleen and Keith stood up shakily to hug him and each other. They were survivors!

Their joy was short-lived. They looked around and saw the mountainside where they stood was no longer a lush green forest; it had become a barren, smoldering landscape of ashes and burning tree stumps, stripped of all life. The air was choked with the overwhelming stench of smoke, so thick that it made their eyes burn.

Kathleen shivered, fighting down the burning feeling in her throat. Pulling her shirt collar up over her nose and mouth, she tried to filter out some of the smoke. "Can we get out of the creek now?" she begged through chattering teeth. "I'm freezing."

"I guess so," her father replied. "But we won't go far until morning, when it's light. We need to be able to see what we're doing."

Wet and shivering, they slowly climbed up the creek-bank and out of the water, dragging their waterlogged sleeping bags with them. Misty followed them, but as soon as her paws touched the scorched ground she yelped and retreated. It was too hot for her to walk on.

"Let's just stay here close to the bank and give everything time to cool down," Mr. Hedges said. He dug around in his backpack and pulled out an aspirin bottle. "We all need to take some of these. Inhaling smoke can give you a bad headache."

Kathleen clutched her stomach. "I don't think I can swallow anything right now, Dad. I'm kind of sick to my stomach."

"Try anyway. We've got a long walk ahead of us tomorrow. You'll need to be in good shape."

Kathleen managed to get the aspirin down with a sip of water, but it didn't last long. She started gagging and then ran over behind a stump to throw up.

"You okay?" Keith asked when she returned.

"I guess," she said wanly. "It's just the *smell!*" Keith and her father were standing next to a burning stump, warming themselves. She quickly joined them. "I feel like I'm never going to be warm again. Funny, after going through a firestorm, huh?"

Keith shifted his weight from one foot to the other. "The only part of me that's warm is my feet," he said. Lifting one foot, he leaned down to examine the bottom of his tennis shoe by the flickering light. "The soles of my shoes are melted!" he said incredulously. "They're all bubbled up."

"You mean my shoes," Kathleen said. "We traded, remember?"

"Oh, yeah."

They decided to find a comfortable place beside the creek and get a few hours sleep. But since their sleeping bags were too damp to get inside, they spent a fitful night shivering.

When the sun finally rose, glaring angrily through the haze, they stood up, cold and cramped. In the bleak daylight their surroundings looked even worse than they had the night before.

Everything was charred, lifeless. Most of the trees were lying on the ground, still smoldering. It was like they imagined the world would appear after a nuclear war.

Kathleen was quiet. She'd spent most of the night throwing up. Her hair and clothes were streaked with greasy black soot; Keith and her father looked just as bad. Sighing, Kathleen dug her toothbrush out of her pack, wanting to get the rancid smoke taste out of her mouth. She stared in surprise: the plastic bristles were all melted together!

Misty sniffed around curiously as they gathered their things, limping slightly. Most of the hair around her paws had been singed off. She was careful not to burn her paws again on the scorched ground.

"Let's go back to the campsite," Mr. Hedges said, pulling on his backpack. "We can pick up anything that's left."

The path was easier to travel now that the thorny underbrush had been burned away. But the thorns had been replaced by a much bigger danger. The trees that were still standing had their roots exposed, like giant fingers disappearing down into the ground; back under those roots fires were still burning, eating away at the trees' foundations. They could fall at any instant.

"Okay, everybody keep a sharp eye out," Mr. Hedges ordered. "If you see a tree falling, just yell 'Forward!' or 'Back!', depending on which way we should all run."

Tramping over burning logs and past charred boulders, they flinched at every cracking sound, afraid it was a tree crashing down on them. The ground was still so hot that if they paused, they had to shift from foot to foot. Misty yelped often as she ran ahead of them, exploring. She found a dead squirrel and nosed it, whining, until Kathleen called her back.

They were glad to reach the campsite. Their plastic groundsheets and bowls were melted, but they were able to salvage most of their pots and pans.

"Let's wait on breakfast till we get back to the bridge," Mr. Hedges said. "Maybe it'll give us somewhere cool to sit."

But when they reached the bridge, all that remained was a charred wooden skeleton. They waded across the stream, finding some rocks on the other side that were cool enough to sit on while they ate. It was hard to believe, looking around, that this was the same lovely spot where they'd met the day before.

Under normal circumstances they could've made it back to the base camp in one day. But now the dangerous conditions slowed them down. Along with watching for falling trees, they also had to keep a close eye on the firestorm's location. It seemed to be heading off to their right, away from them. They decided to follow Horseshoe Creek, hoping to stay by the water as long as they could.

They spotted several live squirrels, but most of the small wildlife they saw was dead: birds, squirrels, even a number of bats. Keith stopped to pick up a particularly crispy bat by the edge of its wing and then held it up in front of Kathleen.

"How do you like your bat?" he said politely. "Rare or well done?"

Kathleen shrieked, "Put it down, Keith! That's disgusting!" He laughed and dropped it.

Suddenly, Kathleen remembered the gold miner they'd seen. "I wonder if that guy with the horses made it out before the firestorm hit?"

"I hope so," Keith said. "I'd hate to find him and his horses out here toasted."

"That's enough, Keith," Mr. Hedges said quickly, seeing the worried look on Kathleen's face. "We don't need that kind of talk."

"Sorry. Anyway, I'm sure he's fine. He was probably on his way out when we saw him."

That afternoon, they could hardly believe their eyes when they looked ahead and saw an oasis of green trees and bushes. After miles and miles of nothing but black, the lush green leaves stood out like beacons. Kathleen and Keith both cheered.

But Mr. Hedges had stopped, frowning. "Be quiet," he said. "I'm trying to listen."

Kathleen and Keith exchanged a puzzled look, but they both fell silent. Then they heard it too—a deep rushing sound, like a distant freight train. Kathleen felt a prickle up her spine. It was the fire!

"Let's move back to where everything's already burned out," Mr. Hedges said. "We'll camp there for the night. By morning we should be able to go on."

They set up a makeshift camp near the stream, cooking dinner over a burning stump. "A pre-built campfire," Keith quipped. "That's one advantage to a forest fire."

"The *only* advantage," Kathleen said. "I'd rather build a fire, thank you."

Night had fallen when they saw a bobbing light approaching. It turned out to be a muscular young man with a German shepherd. The dog was carrying its own small backpack. Kathleen grabbed Misty.

"Hi!" the man said. "Mind if I join you folks?"

"Not at all," Mr. Hedges said. "Were you caught in the firestorm last night?"

"No, they've closed all the trails that are dangerous."

The man introduced himself as Tom Sewell, a teacher. He ended up camping with them overnight. By the time they got up the next morning, though, he and his dog were already gone. As a parting gesture, he had set their pan of water near the fire to heat up.

They headed out right after breakfast, determined to make it back to their base camp that day. The fire had consumed the green area from the day before, leaving it as black and lifeless as the rest of the burned-out forest. They could now safely pass through.

The next time they reached a green area, there was no ominous rushing of wind to turn them back. They walked on, enjoying the cool, springy feeling of the grass and pine needles beneath their feet.

Late that afternoon they reached the steep area Kathleen and Keith had climbed down in the beginning on their way to the trail. Weary, their half-melted shoes barely hanging on their feet, they started up the slope.

They'd only gone a short way when a Sheriff's Department jeep drove up and stopped next to them. "You folks the Hedges?" the deputy asked.

"Yes," Mr. Hedges replied.

"A hiker came into town this morning and said you were out here. Thought you might need help."

"Thanks. Our camp site is on the other side of this ridge. If you could just give us a ride to the top, it would be a big help."

"No problem. Hop in!"

* * *

Back at the camp, Mrs. Hedges was busily preparing a big batch of spareribs for dinner. These last two days had been rough; she'd been unable to shake off the feeling that something was terribly wrong. To calm her nerves, she and the children had gone into town that day to look around.

Now, brushing sauce over the ribs, she wondered why she had made so much food. Pat and the kids weren't due back for three more days. The ribs would go to waste. Suddenly, she became aware of a rancid smoke odor, like old cigarettes. "Mom!" Angie exclaimed. "Look behind you!"

Whirling around, Mrs. Hedges saw three people and a dog approaching, all of them covered with soot. She stared in alarm until the man said with a grin, "You weren't going to eat those spareribs without me, were you?" It was her husband!

Later, after the three weary adventurers scrubbed themselves repeatedly with hot soapy water, they sat down to dinner. Between bites, they took turns telling what had happened.

Mrs. Hedges listened, shaking her head. "I kept having this horrible feeling," she said. "I even woke up night before last thinking somebody was calling me. I sat up for the longest time after that."

Kathleen was reminded of the moment when, in deepest despair, she'd thought about how sad her mother would be to lose them. Had her silent cry somehow reached her ear?

Late that night, after everyone else had fallen asleep, Kathleen and Keith sat up talking. The events of the last few days had left them both shaken. It was strange to realize that all their bright dreams of the future could have ended in a single moment.

"I promised God I'd be a better person if he let us make it," Keith confessed. "It's crazy, the stuff you think at times like that."

"I know. It still seems so unreal. I keep thinking that we could be dead right now! It gives you a funny feeling." She was quiet for a moment. "It sounds weird, but I think it really was God who saved us."

Keith looked at her. "Yeah, I guess I do, too." He sounded surprised.

They finally settled back to go to sleep. The whole family would be packing up to leave the area first thing in the morning. They'd decided to spend the rest of their vacation in a less exciting spot.

"Kathleen?" Keith said in the darkness.

"Mm?"

"I'm glad you're not dead."

Kathleen grinned at her brother's awkward tone. "I'm glad you're not dead, too," she said kindly. "I was just thinking, I'd get awfully lonely living on that tropical island all by myself."

Plane Crash on Christmas Day

The Shawna Trantham Story

Thirteen-year-old Shawna Trantham shoved her foot down into one of her brand new lace-up boots, enjoying the rich leather smell. It had been a great Christmas 1992 after all, she thought as she leaned down to tie the laces, an awkward task with her left arm in a cast. Her wrist had been broken several weeks before when she was bucked off a horse at a friend's grandad's farm.

She stood up to admire herself in the mirror. Tall, sturdy, with curly reddish-brown hair, she looked every inch a hardy West Texas girl. She grinned at her reflection, liking the effect of her new jeans and the boots. Too bad Kenneth couldn't come over today to see her!

She went to the kitchen, stiff boots creaking with each step. Her older brother, Anthony, was sitting at the table.

"Hey," she greeted him. "Check this out!" She pranced in a small circle to show off the outfit. "What do you think?"

"Uh-huh," Anthony said. He was a man of few words.

She looked in the refrigerator and then tried again. "You want to try out Mom and Dad's new juicer? There're some grapes and stuff in here we can squish up."

Anthony shrugged. "Okay, but Mom's gone to work. Can you believe they're making her work on Christmas?"

LaFonda Trantham was a nurse. "Yeah, it stinks. She's got to work the early shift tomorrow, too. I bet we'll have to leave Aunt Gator's early so Mom can get some sleep."

"Aunt Gator" was really Aunt LaGaytha, their mother's sister. With her fluffy blond hair and bright blue eyes she didn't look the least bit like an alligator, but the nickname had started when she was a child. The way Pa Thompson told it, LaGaytha had been trying to fit a huge spoonful of frosting into her mouth one day when he'd looked over and laughed. "With your mouth wide open like that, you look just like a gator!" he'd told her. From that day on, LaGaytha was "Gator."

Shawna used her good arm to slide the heavy stainless steel juicer out of its box and set it on the counter. She and Anthony had bought it for their parents that Christmas, impressed by its claims to make "healthful, delicious juices." She scanned the instructions.

"Okay," she said. "We're supposed to wash the fruit and just dump it in. That sounds easy enough."

Anthony handed her a couple of oranges, a handful of grapes, and an apple. She rinsed them and dropped them into the juicer. Anthony peered down at the colorful jumble doubtfully. "Shouldn't we at least peel the oranges?" he asked.

"It says not to." She clamped the lid down. "The peels have extra vitamins or something. Ready?"

"I guess."

She jabbed a red button and the juicer sprang to life, roaring and churning like a small garbage truck. Shawna counted to thirty, turned it off, and then lifted the top. The liquid inside looked a little strange, but sort of juice-like.

"Dad!" she yelled over her shoulder. "C'mere!" When he wandered in, she filled a glass for him. "It's your juicer, so we thought you should be the first one to try it."

Mr. Trantham stared down at the lumpy orange-colored juice. "What's in this?" he asked suspiciously.

"Oh, just oranges and stuff. Go ahead, try it!"

Shawna watched eagerly as he lifted the glass to his lips. His reaction—a long, shuddering flinch—wasn't encouraging.

"Here, let me try it," Anthony said manfully. He took the glass, sipped, and then whirled around to spit it out into the sink. "Yuck!" he sputtered. "That's horrible!"

Shawna laughed. "It can't be all that bad. It's just fruit." She took the glass and sipped gingerly. The juice tasted nasty, bitter, and kind of *stringy.* She made a face and swallowed quickly.

"Okay, it's bad," she admitted. "*Really* bad." They poured the rest down the sink.

The rest of Christmas Day turned out, as always, to be boring. Most of Shawna and Anthony's friends were either out of town or with their families. They finally walked to the park across the street to play basketball, trying to kill time until they left for Aunt Gator's. The whole family was gathering there for a big Christmas dinner.

After they got bored with basketball, Shawna wandered back to her room and plopped on her bed. Even if Kenneth couldn't come over, maybe she could talk to him on the phone. She punched in his number. After two rings Kenneth's familiar voice drawled, "Hello?"

"It's me." Kenneth was her boyfriend—sort of—and they could talk for hours without running out of things to say. They chatted comfortably for a few minutes, comparing their "Christmas loot."

"Wait till you see my new boots," Shawna bragged, admiring their two-toned beauty as she spoke. She frowned when she noticed a small scuff mark on her left toe, and leaned down to rub at it. "They're to-o-o cool. I got new jeans, too."

When they exhausted Christmas as a topic, they switched easily to sports. They had a long-standing feud about whether the Boston Celtics or the Charlotte Hornets were the best basketball team. Shawna was a firm Celtics fan.

"Larry Bird is incredible," she said. "The Hornets don't have anybody even close. Pa-the-tic!" She grinned at Kenneth's indignant squawk, remembering how he'd protested when she'd made all her friends at school sign her white cast in green ink—the Celtics' colors. She'd gotten a new cast a few weeks before, covered in bright red material decorated with little Frosty the Snowmen.

Finally, her father stuck his head in the door to announce that it was time to go. Aunt Gator lived in Lake Ransom Canyon, about forty minutes away. Mrs. Trantham would be driving out to join them as soon as her shift ended at the hospital.

It was a little before four o'clock when they pulled into the driveway of Aunt Gator's comfortable brown brick house. Jenelle, eleven, immediately flung open the door. "Shawna!" she yelled happily. "Hey, Mom, they're here!"

Aunt Gator appeared as they trooped up to the door. "Come on in!" she said, beaming as she hugged them one by one. "Dinner's waiting."

Shawna and Jenelle, closest in age among all the cousins, bounced inside together talking happily. Jenelle's parents were separated, and her father, Jim Fitzgerald, had flown up from Houston that day in his single-engine Piper Cherokee to visit for the holiday. He grinned and waved to Shawna and Anthony from across the room. Granny Thompson, plump and smiling, swept

Shawna up into a warm, flower-scented hug and passed her on to Pa Thompson, who gave her a quick squeeze and scratchy kiss on the cheek. Colin and Heather, Jenelle's older brother and sister, called out their greetings. Anthony went over to join them and their friends.

Shawna sighed, glad to be through the relative "hug-a-thon." "So, Jenelle," she said, straightening her new shirt, "what've you been up to lately?"

Her cousin shrugged, tossing her long blond hair. "Nothing much—just school and stuff. How about you?"

Shawna held up her cast. "I haven't been able to do a whole lot since this happened."

"Hey, did you hear that my dad might be taking some of us up in his plane later? If he does, you want to come?"

"Sure! I've never been in a plane before."

"I have been, lots of times. It's fun."

Mrs. Trantham arrived a few minutes later, still wearing her nurse's uniform. She looked tired, but she quickly brightened as she greeted her sister and the rest of the family. Aunt Gator pointed to the buffet table, her blue eyes twinkling.

"Mom brought that delicious gelatin salad again this year," she said. "But I'm planning to eat it all myself."

Mrs. Trantham grinned. "Not if I get to it first!" Laughing, the two sisters raced for the table.

Shawna, watching, shook her head. "I guess I'd better go get some food before my mother eats it all."

Shawna ate quickly, anxious to get to the next part of the Christmas tradition—exchanging gifts with the rest of the family. But as always, her mom and dad liked to linger over the meal, probably just to torture her and Anthony. It was almost dark by the time they finished.

The twinkling Christmas tree was standing in the living room next to the fireplace. "Okay," Aunt Gator said, "I guess we can go ahead and exchange presents now. Unless the kids want to wait a little longer—"

"Mom!" Jenelle said impatiently. "Let's just do it!"

Aunt Gator leaned down to select the first gift. "Anthony, it looks like this one's yours." She handed it to him and then chose the next one. Before long the sounds of ripping paper and laughter filled the room.

Shawna opened hers to find a new nightgown decorated with a solemn looking cat. She held it up against her. "I needed a new nightgown. Mine are all old and ratty. Thanks a lot, Aunt Gator!"

"You're welcome, hon. Hope it fits."

They were all still admiring each other's gifts when Uncle Jim stood up and stretched. "I'm going to take the plane up to check out the Christmas lights over the canyon," he announced. "Who wants to come along?"

Shawna, Jenelle, and most of the other kids chorused, "I do!" Uncle Jim laughed.

"I can only take three at a time. Shawna, I know your mom needs to get back home early tonight, so why don't you and Jenelle come first? LaGaytha, you can copilot for me."

"As long as I don't have to do any of the flying," she laughed.

Night Flight

The airport was about ten miles away. When they arrived, Shawna hopped out of the car and walked over to Uncle Jim's plane, examining it with interest. It was cream-colored with a brown stripe down the side. There was a single propeller on its nose.

"Can I ride up front, Uncle Jim?" she asked. "Please?"

Aunt Gator quickly shook her head. "Sorry, hon, but I get airsick. You wouldn't want me sitting behind you. Trust me."

Shawna laughed. "N-o-o problem. I'd *much* rather ride in the back with Jenelle."

Aunt Gator grinned. "I thought you'd feel that way."

Uncle Jim unlocked the plane and helped both girls up. They ducked through the low doorway and squeezed back into the cramped back seats.

"I'd always imagined planes were bigger than this," Shawna said, sliding her feet under her seat. Her knees were still almost touching the back of Aunt Gator's seat.

"It *is* pretty small," Jenelle agreed, and then added, "Your seat belt's behind you somewhere. You need to put it on."

Shawna groped around, found the belt and then hooked it across her lap with a metallic click. Somehow, the sound made her nervous.

Uncle Jim was strapping into the pilot's seat. "Everybody buckled up back there?" he asked.

"Yeah, we're ready!" Jenelle answered.

"Then let's get this crate in the air!" Uncle Jim flipped several switches. The engine instantly roared to life, causing the small plane to shudder convulsively. Shawna watched, wide-eyed, as he checked all the gauges and then spoke crisply into the radio. It all seemed so scary!

Jenelle noticed Shawna's silence. "Hey, don't be *nervous*," she said, teasing. "It's not like we crash *every* time."

Shawna rolled her eyes. "Right, Jenelle." Still, as the plane lurched forward, her stomach tensed. She'd somehow imagined it would feel more stable, like a car driving down the highway.

They taxied to the end of the runway and paused again while Uncle Jim did a few more last-minute checks. He pulled a small knob on the control panel, making the vibrating roar of the engine grow even louder and more violent. It felt as if the whole plane was going to shake apart before they even got off the ground!

Then, with one swift movement, Uncle Jim released the brake. The small plane shot forward, gaining speed as it bumped rapidly over the concrete runway. Shawna gasped and gripped the armrests tightly. Within seconds they were going eighty miles per hour.

But the jolting ride ended abruptly as the plane left the ground, sweeping up into the clear night sky. Shawna relaxed and let her breath out slowly.

"How you doing, Shawna?" Aunt Gator yelled over her shoulder.

"Fine!" she replied. She stared out the small window, fascinated. Even though they were still climbing, she could see for miles. The flat, cactus-dotted West Texas landscape stretched out endlessly, broken up by clusters of tiny houses that looked like Monopoly pieces. The highway slithered along far below them like a snake.

Her aunt pointed just ahead and to the right. "We're coming up on the canyon now. See? Those lights are some of the houses along the rim."

Shawna gazed down at the twinkling clusters of lights. "This is awesome!" she said. She continued to stare as they started out over the canyon—a dark, jagged gorge almost two miles across. In the pale moonlight the wide, shadowy crevices among the broken boulders below looked almost bottomless. She pressed her forehead against the window so she could see better, feeling the buzzing vibration of the engine in the cool glass.

Then suddenly, without warning, the vibration stopped. In the sudden silence, the small plane dipped with a sickening lurch. Shawna whirled toward Jenelle, eyes wide, but her cousin wasn't smiling. What was happening?

Uncle Jim was flipping one switch after another, trying to restart the engine. He finally banked the plane hard to the left, heading back toward the highway. "Something's wrong," he said. "We've got to go back."

Aunt Gator stared over at him. "Stop kidding around, Jimmy. This isn't funny!"

"I'm not joking!" he snapped. "We're in big trouble."

Shawna sat, frozen, as she took in her uncle's chilling words. Despite the coolness of the night, she could see beads of sweat forming on Uncle Jim's forehead as he fought with the controls, trying to keep the plane as high as possible. If they could just circle back around and clear the gaping canyon, there were plenty of flat fields along the rim where they could safely land.

But the heavy downward glide of the plane was too much to overcome. As they sank lower and lower, the sheer walls of the canyon rose all around them, seeming to swallow them. In the glare of the landing lights, they saw a rocky ridge looming directly ahead.

"Jimmy, we're going to hit it!" Aunt Gator screamed.

Shawna pressed her body back into her seat, too terrified to even scream. *This is it,* she thought. *We're all going to die.* Jenelle burst into hysterical tears. "Help us, Lord Jesus!" she sobbed. "Please help us!"

Uncle Jim continued to fight the controls, trying desperately to ease the sinking plane past the ridge. Then he spotted a tiny, somewhat level clearing along the slope directly below them. Although it was barely the size of a house, it was their only chance.

"Brace yourselves!" he shouted. Grabbing the control stick, he broke the plane out of its sharp turn and then pointed its nose almost straight down toward the clearing. The small craft dropped out from under them like a falling elevator, spiraling down . . . down . . . down . . .

The last sounds Shawna heard were her cousin's sobs and her aunt's terrified screams. Then the Piper Cherokee nosed with explosive impact into the sheer, stony slope near the bottom of Ransom Canyon.

Struggle for Survival

Mrs. Trantham shook her head firmly when her mother urged her to take another piece of pie.

"I'm stuffed!" she protested, laughing. "I can't eat another bite. As it is I'm probably going to have to buy a bigger uniform." She glanced at the clock on the mantle, surprised to see it was already almost nine. "Hey, shouldn't the kids be back by now? I need to get home."

At that instant, distant sirens suddenly sprang to life. Mrs. Trantham and her mother exchanged a startled look and then ran outside into the yard. Gazing across the flat Texas plain, they saw an ominous string of police cars, ambulances, and fire trucks heading east along the far-off highway, red and blue lights flashing.

Mrs. Trantham felt a sudden dark foreboding. "Mom!" she said urgently. "Which way is the airport?"

Granny's plump face suddenly looked pinched as she lifted her hand—and mutely pointed east.

* * *

Shawna groaned. Why was she so cold? With a great effort she opened her eyes, but at first she couldn't make much sense of her confusing surroundings. She seemed to be huddled in the dark in a half-sitting position, her left arm pinned against her side. Both her legs were also stuck. There was an odd smell in the air that burned her eyes and nose, and nearby someone was moaning softly. A red light was flashing every few seconds, piercing the darkness. What was going on?

The plane had crashed.

The realization sent a sudden wave of panic washing over Shawna. How long had she been sitting there? Where were the others? After trying in vain to free her legs from the jumbled wreckage, she leaned forward to peer out the gaping hole where the passenger door had been—now level with the ground. A shadowy figure was sitting just outside, his back to the plane.

"Uncle Jim!" she shrieked. Her uncle turned his head toward her, but he didn't speak. She held out her right hand toward him. "Pull me out! My other arm's stuck!"

He stared at her, dazed. "I can't," he mumbled. His voice sounded distant, as if he didn't know what he was saying. In the flickering light of the plane's beacon, she saw his face was cut and bloody. His right arm hung limply at his side, and his right leg appeared to be twisted at an odd angle. His breath was coming in short gasps.

"Uncle Jim!" Shawna wailed, starting to cry. "You've got to! Come on! Just do it!"

Her hysterical tone seemed to cut through his confusion. With a low moan he leaned back on the ground to get closer and then reached up toward her with his good arm. Shawna stretched forward and grabbed his hand.

"Now *pull!*" she pleaded.

With her uncle's help, she managed to kick and squirm her way out of the jumbled wreckage and crawl up into the front seat. But once there, Shawna stared in horror: her aunt's limp body was hanging halfway out the passenger door, her legs still pinned inside the plane.

Her face, resting on the stony ground outside, was bloody and almost unrecognizable. Shawna would have to crawl over her to get out.

"Aunt Gator, are you okay?" she asked tearfully. Her aunt just moaned. Shawna tried to crawl around her aunt without stepping on her. She felt as if she were trapped in a nightmare.

Once outside, she stood up shakily and looked around. Uncle Jim was sitting up again, still acting dazed. She was relieved to find Jenelle huddled under the plane's broken wing, crying softly. Her younger cousin's face was pouring blood, and something was wrong with her left leg. But she was *alive*!

Shawna forced herself to calm down and think clearly. What would they do on "Rescue 9-1-1"?

They'd call an ambulance, she thought. *But I don't have a phone. There's got to be some other way to get help.*

"Uncle Jim!" she said. "Where are we?"

He paused and answered helplessly, "I don't know."

Shawna looked around the dark, sprawling canyon, her heart sinking as she saw the impossibly steep slopes rising on every side. They were miles from anywhere. She looked at her aunt and uncle and then at Jenelle. If they were to survive, they needed help *fast*.

"I'm going for help," she announced, not sure if any of them even understood. "I love you."

She paused, trying to decide which way to go. Far off to the left, high above them, she caught a glimpse of what looked like tiny headlights moving along. The highway!

She'd only taken a few steps in that direction, though, when something caused her to hesitate. She glanced down—then gasped. Another step and she would've walked right off the edge of a sheer twenty-five-foot drop-off! Heart pounding, she turned around and went the opposite direction. She'd have to climb out the long way and then circle back around to the highway.

The canyon bottom, rippled with dozens of steep ridges, was strewn with rough boulders and cactus clumps, a brutal obstacle course to cross in the dark. As Shawna stumbled along, her new boots slipping on the loose red soil, she gradually noticed the tinny taste of blood in her mouth. For the first time she realized that she, too, might've been injured in the crash.

She touched her face gingerly, feeling the slippery wetness of blood. Her nose and lips were swollen and split; her chin was deeply gashed. Blood was dripping down steadily onto her new shirt, which was ripped in several places.

But it wasn't until she looked down at her left arm that she got scared. Cast and all, her arm dangled loosely from her shoulder at an odd angle. She couldn't even feel it. It didn't seem to be attached to her body any longer. Frightened, she cradled it in her other arm and hurried on.

She worked her way over the steep ridges, using her good arm to help claw her way up each slope. Several times she slipped and fell with jarring impact, landing on her hurt arm.

After what seemed an eternity of walking, climbing, and falling, her strength began to wane. Was she even going in the right direction anymore? Each time she fell, it was harder to get back up. It would feel so good to rest for a while, to lay back and look up at the stars.

Every time, however, the images of Aunt Gator, Uncle Jim, and Jenelle rose to Shawna's mind, bringing her struggling back to her feet. They'd die if she quit. She had to keep going.

Somehow, she made it all the way across the canyon bottom. But now she faced the most difficult task of all—climbing to the top of the rim. Shawna stopped, her stomach knotting as she looked up the steep, rocky slope. She couldn't possibly make it. She was too exhausted, too weak. It couldn't be done.

She started up the slope.

Clawing at the rocks and dry grass, she worked her way upward foot by foot. She'd climbed about fifteen feet when her boot slipped, sending her tumbling backward in a shower of gravel. She landed hard on her stomach back at the bottom of the slope.

Gasping for breath, Shawna felt hot tears welling in her eyes. It had taken everything she had to make that last attempt. Maybe it was shock or loss of blood or just the frigid night air, but she had no strength left. She pressed her face against the cold, damp ground and began to cry.

"I can't do it," she sobbed, hardly knowing what she was saying. "I need help. Please help me!"

Suddenly, she felt an infusion of strength rippling through her body like electricity. Energy surged back into her and a comforting sense of warmth, just as if someone had wrapped her in a blanket. She rested for a moment and then slowly stood up, astonished at how little effort it took. What had happened?

Glancing up at the stars twinkling overhead, she suddenly remembered what day it was. Christmas Day. Was this some kind of gift to her, a gift of strength when she needed it most?

She eyed the slope with new determination. Somehow, she was going to do it! Without hesitation she started scrambling up. In less than five minutes she was standing at the top.

"I made it!" she said incredulously. But her excitement was short-lived. Instead of being near a road or houses, she was surrounded by dark, empty fields. The faint glimmer of headlights from the highway were still far off to her left—and all the way across the sprawling canyon. She still had a long way to go.

Because of the canyon's jagged shape, she thought it might be quickest to circle around to the right, so Shawna set off again into the darkness. The ground along the rim was rough, but it was somewhat level. She held her left arm tightly to keep it from swinging around.

After almost thirty minutes, she reached a barbed-wire fence along what looked like another empty field. She crossed the fence without hesitation. It was probably private property, but this was an emergency.

She'd only taken a few steps when she saw headlights moving along not far ahead. She stared, uncomprehending, and then started running. There must be a road!

"Hey!" she screamed, dropping her left arm so she could wave with her right. "Stop! I need help!"

By the time she got there, however, the cars had already flashed past. They hadn't even noticed her small, desperate figure approaching in the darkness.

Stumbling onto the pavement, Shawna sobbed with disappointment as she watched the red taillights disappear into the distance. If only she had gotten there a few seconds earlier!

Suddenly, she noticed a flicker of light behind her.

Another car! Planting herself in the middle of the road, she jumped up and down and waved frantically, determined this time not to be missed. The approaching car slowed down, pinioning her for a moment in its headlights, but it didn't stop. Crying hysterically, Shawna ran over into the next lane to keep from being run down.

"Help!" she pleaded as the car drove past, its occupants staring at her. "Please don't leave me! *Please!*"

Then the car's brake lights went on. As it rolled to a stop, Shawna ran up to the driver's door, barely able to talk through her tears. The driver, an older man, rolled down his window.

"What happened?" he asked, taking in Shawna's torn and bloody clothes. He was stunned by her response.

"There's been a plane crash!" she sobbed. "Please, I need to get help for the others!"

Canyon Rescue

Mrs. Trantham and her mother sped to the airport, praying that they were imagining things. But when they arrived, they discovered that their fears were justified. People there had watched Jimmy's plane take off and fly up over the canyon and then start to circle back when it dropped out of sight. So far, they hadn't reappeared.

Mrs. Trantham felt her mouth go dry. "I'm going over there," she said.

By now, emergency helicopters were slicing through the dark night sky toward Ransom Canyon, their search lights criss-crossing the rugged terrain below. As she approached the mouth of the canyon, Mrs. Trantham spotted a group of police cars. She pulled over and got out. The first thing she saw as she peered down into the canyon was the flashing beacon light of a small airplane—crumpled on the ground.

She ran up to a police officer. "My daughter, my niece, and my sister and brother-in-law were all in that plane," she said. "I'm a nurse. Do you know if they're okay?"

At that moment, a police scanner nearby crackled to life: *"Girl involved in plane crash en route to Methodist Hospital. Father has been notified."*

Mrs. Trantham's eyes widened. "Who is she?" she asked urgently. "The girl from the crash—does she have a cast on her arm?"

"I don't know," the officer said, "but I can sure find out." Speaking into the radio, he asked several questions and then turned back to Mrs. Trantham. "She does have a cast. It's on her left arm. They say she climbed out of the canyon to get help for the others. She flagged down some people driving by."

Mrs. Trantham bit her lip, tears flooding her eyes. "That's Shawna, my daughter." The policeman smiled. "Sounds like a pretty spunky kid."

Largely thanks to Shawna's quick action, her aunt, uncle, and cousin all survived. Uncle Jim suffered the worst injuries: he broke his right arm and leg, eight of his ribs, punctured one of his lungs, and also suffered severe internal and head injuries. He remained unconscious in the hospital for over two months, but did eventually recover enough to go home.

Aunt Gator had several broken vertebrae, a broken nose, ankle, and rib, along with two broken legs. Jenelle escaped with a cut face and one broken leg. They also both recovered.

As for Shawna, she wasn't surprised to learn at the hospital that she'd re-broken her left wrist and added a new break up above her cast, close to her shoulder—not bad, all things considered. Although she was weak and shaky for a few days, she was soon well enough to go home.

One of the first things she did was call Kenneth.

"It all seems sort of unreal now," she said after reliving the whole story with him. She was propped up comfortably on pillows, her left arm encased in a heavy cast. "It's like I didn't really even know what I was doing, especially there at the end. I still don't understand how I made it up that last slope." She shook her head, remembering. "Anyway," she continued, "I can tell you one thing. Next year, if anybody wants to go look at Christmas lights, I'm going to make sure they're staying on the ground. I sure wouldn't want this to become some kind of family Christmas tradition!"

Shawna Trantham and her brother Anthony

Photo: Stan Bell

Lost in Hidden Treasure Mine

The Josh Dennis Story

Josh Dennis lay motionless on his stomach in the tall, prickly grass, holding his breath as he squinted down the barrel of his wooden rifle. He sighted in on a tiny spot on top of the next small hill. *Any second now,* he thought, ignoring a gnat buzzing near his left ear. *Come on. Come on!*

Suddenly, a loud *pow!* directly behind him made him yelp in surprise. He whirled to face Terry Nelson, a grinning twelve-year-old holding a smoking cap gun.

51

"Aw," Josh said in disgust, jumping up to dust the dried grass off his pants. "How'd you get behind me so quick? I thought you guys would sneak over the hill."

It was a hot July day in northern Utah; Josh, a cheerful, blond ten-year-old, was making the most of the remaining summer of 1989 with his two best friends from the neighborhood. The large empty lot behind their subdivision made a perfect battlefield for their noisy games of "army" and football.

Terry said smugly, "We split up and circled around behind you. Hey, Kirk, come on out! I got him!"

Cutting between the houses back toward Josh's street a few minutes later, the three boys laughed and shoved each other, Terry and Kirk still relishing their victory. Josh led them into his house, calling cheerfully, "Mom, I'm home!"

Without waiting for a reply he led the troops into the kitchen. "You guys want some Tin Roof Sundae™ ice cream?"

"Sure!" they chorused. They were busy scooping it into bowls when Josh's mom, Janeen, walked in, her light brown hair swinging loose around her shoulders. She smiled when she saw the boys hovering over the ice cream carton like three hungry vultures.

"Hey!" she said in mock protest. "What do you think this is, an ice cream parlor?"

Josh grinned. "Yep!" He ducked as she took a playful swipe at him before she hurried through the kitchen into the laundry room.

The oldest of four kids in his family, Joshua Dennis was small for his age, about the same size as Kirk, who was a whole year younger. But although he got teased sometimes about his size, he had never let it stop him. Fast and wiry, he often competed and won against much bigger kids in sports and games—like the week before, when he hit his first-ever home run.

He'd never forget that day. His Little League team, the Braves, was losing three to one when he stepped up to bat, sweating as much from nervousness as from the heat. It was near the end of the game, and his team already had two outs. Now they had two men on base. If he hit the ball he'd be a hero; if he didn't, they were almost sure to lose.

The pitcher began his windup, and Josh tensed, his eyes on the ball. An instant later he heard it thud into the catcher's mitt just behind him.

"Striiiiike one!" the umpire shouted. The opposing team cheered. His own teammates groaned.

Josh shuffled his feet nervously, adjusted his batting helmet, and tightened his grip on the bat. But once again, he didn't even have time to take a swing at the ball before it whizzed by.

"Strike two!" Behind him, Josh could hear the disappointed mutters of his teammates. Across the field, someone on the other team jeered, "Keep it up, Number Four! You're doing great!" He forced himself to block it all out as he lifted the bat again, determined to swing this time no matter what.

The pitcher released the ball, and it hurtled straight for the plate. Holding his breath, Josh stepped forward and leaned into the swing—and felt the bat connect solidly with the ball!

It shot straight into the outfield. Josh dropped his bat and took off, his cleats pounding the dirt as he rounded first, then second.

"Keep going, Josh!" his coach screamed. "All the way!"

Heart pounding, Josh ran across third and then raced for home. His breath was coming in short gasps by the time he flew across home plate—and straight into the arms of his ecstatic teammates.

They'd won the game that day 4 to 3.

Now, scarfing ice cream with Terry and Kirk, Josh tried not to think about school starting again in just a few more weeks. Terry would be going off to junior high while Josh and Kirk remained at Fox Hill Elementary. It just wouldn't be the same.

Josh sighed. "You guys want to go skateboarding for a while?" he asked, carrying his ice cream bowl to the sink and swishing water in it before shoving it into the dishwasher with a clank. "Can we use your ramp, Terry?"

Terry nodded, and they all swooped back out of the house, slamming the door behind them.

When Josh got home, it was already dinnertime. He washed his hands and hurriedly slid into his place at the table. It was two-year-old Jake's turn to ask the blessing.

He did it in his own rambling fashion. "T'ank you f'r Mommy and Daddy and Joshie and Danielle and Terra," he prayed sincerely—only he pronounced his sister's name "Tewwa"—"and f'r my room and Striper and Mommy and Daddy and—"

Josh rolled his eyes impatiently; the little goof was starting all over again! When Jake paused for breath he hastily interrupted. "Amen," he said loudly.

"Amen," the rest of the family murmured. Although his mother cast him a slightly reproachful glance, Josh could tell she wasn't really mad. She probably wanted to eat as much as he did.

"So what'd you kids do all day?" asked Terry Dennis. It was kind of funny that his father and best friend had the same first name, but since Josh called his dad "Dad" he guessed it wasn't too confusing.

Seven-year-old Danielle answered first. "I went over to Jenny's house," she said, brushing her wispy blond hair back from her face, "and we played Barbie and watched *Cinderella!*"

"And Daddy!" five-year-old Terra blurted out. "I put *The Neverending Story* into the VCR today, and I didn't even break it!"

She looked offended when the rest of the family burst out laughing. In the last year alone, Terra had managed to destroy two VCRs by accidentally knocking them off the top of the television.

"That's good, honey," her dad said in amusement. "I'm proud of you." Then he turned to Josh. "You're being awfully quiet over there, son. What've these women been doing to you?"

"Nothing. I just hung around with Terry and Kirk all day. You know, skateboarding and stuff."

"Sounds like fun. But you must be getting pretty tired of all this playing around by now, huh? Probably can't wait for school to start." Josh groaned, and his father grinned. "Oh, well, at least you've still got something to look forward to. We've got almost thirty boys signed up for the big camping trip in September."

Mr. Dennis, an assistant bureau chief with the state's Criminal Identification Division, was also a Boy Scout leader. Even though Josh was still officially a Webelos Scout, his dad sometimes let him go along on trips with the older Scouts in Troop 845.

"Yeah, well, that'll be pretty cool," Josh admitted, "especially since Terry Nelson gets to go this time."

The next few weeks flew by, and almost before Josh knew it school was starting. On the first day of the new year, Kirk was waiting outside for him, and they began the twenty-minute walk to Fox Hills Elementary. As the two friends started down the sidewalk together, they both were glum.

"Who do you have this year?" Kirk asked. "I've got Mrs. Olsen."

"I've got Mrs. Mills," Josh replied. "Everybody says she's really mean." He made a face.

Laughing, they veered off the sidewalk to take a shortcut between the houses to get to the kittywalk, a kind of fenced-in bridge leading to the next neighborhood. When they reached the school, they saw the noisy mob of children and parents gathered outside the front door.

Josh spotted a tall boy with glasses across the schoolyard. "Hey, Dustin!" he shouted. "Over here!" Dustin waved and walked toward him, and a moment later they were talking happily. They were glad to discover they were in the same class.

A few minutes later, when the warning bell rang, Josh waved at Kirk. "See you after school!" he shouted. He and Dustin raced to Mrs. Mills' room to claim desks beside each other. They settled in, arranging their school supplies as they greeted other classmates. Mrs. Mills walked by and smiled, looking distinctly *un*-mean. Maybe fifth grade wasn't going to be so bad after all!

The next few days dragged by, but finally it was Friday again. Josh ran all the way home after school. He was standing on the front porch when the neighbor down the street pulled up in her white mini-van. Danielle jumped out and bounced up the walk, swinging her bright pink lunch box.

Josh grinned. "I beat you home, and I didn't get a ride!"

Danielle made a face as she brushed past him into the house. "Who cares? I think it's stupid to walk all that way when you could ride!"

Hearing their voices, Jake charged into the living room as fast as his short, chubby legs could carry him. He paused to hug Danielle and then said gleefully, "Joshie!" He held his arms up to be picked up.

Josh grinned and scooped him up, settling him on one hip. "Hey, bud! Give me five!" Jake giggled and slapped his big brother's open palm with his own tiny hand before wriggling away.

Josh fixed himself a quick snack and then went back to his bedroom to feed his hamster. When he reached into the cage, though, Striper didn't run to his hand like usual. Josh frowned, digging down into the cardboard-like litter to scoop him up. The hamster huddled on his palm, his sides heaving.

"Hey, what's the matter with you?" Josh asked, stroking the small animal's soft brown and white fur. Striper was twitching in a strange way.

Alarmed, he stuck his head out the door. "Mom! C'mere, quick! Something's wrong with Striper!"

Mrs. Dennis hurried into his room, drying her hands on a dish towel. "What's the matter?"

"Look!" Josh held up the hamster, hunched miserably on his palm. "He's acting really funny. I think he's sick."

Mrs. Dennis leaned close and stroked Striper gently with one finger. "He really doesn't look too good, does he?" She hesitated. "You know, honey, Striper's getting to be a pretty old hamster. It might just be that—"

"No! He's been fine until today. He's just sick."

"All right, all right. Maybe he caught a cold or something. Let's keep a close eye on him for a few days and see how he does."

Josh lowered the hamster back into the wire cage, trying not to jostle him. Striper immediately burrowed down deep in the litter and hid there, quivering. Despite his confident words, Josh was suddenly afraid. What if Striper *was* dying?

He shook off the thought. He had homework to do. Switching on his radio, he dug around in his junk drawer for a pencil. He had to stir around a bunch of toy cars, broken Transformers,™ baseball cards, marbles, and about a hundred candy wrappers before emerging victoriously with a short pencil stub. He plopped down in his desk chair, tilted it back, and pulled his notebook onto his lap.

The small bedroom, which he shared with Jake, was cluttered with a tangle of clothes, toys, and books. Josh had tried briefly to decorate the room by covering the walls with posters, but there was only so much he could do. His favorite poster was the Batman one he'd gotten after going to see the movie. He planned to be Batman that Halloween.

He was frowning over his math homework a few minutes later when Terra ran in, as usual without knocking. "What's the matter with Striper?" she asked breathlessly. "Mom said he's sick. Can I see him?"

Josh glared. "Mom! Will you tell Terra to quit coming into my room? And make her leave my hamster alone."

"Terra!" His mom's voice sounded far away. "Leave your brother alone."

"You heard her. Get out!" Josh ordered.

Terra pouted. "Okay, okay. I just wanted to know what was wrong with your dumb old hamster."

Josh waited until she was almost out of earshot, then muttered, "He may be dumb, but he's still smarter than *you*." He grinned when she flounced angrily toward the kitchen complaining, "Mo-om!"

Sisters! he thought.

The Big Campout Approaches

That weekend was busy. Josh and his dad were trying to get ready for the big Scout outing the next weekend; the rest of the family were cleaning the house, getting ready for the painters who were coming.

"Why do you keep telling me to clean my room?" Josh grumbled for the hundredth time. "It *is* clean!"

Mrs. Dennis looked at him in exasperation. "I want you to *really* clean, not just kick everything out of sight. We'll be moving the furniture around, and I don't want to find any old socks or dirty underwear under your bed. I think you and your hamster both would be perfectly happy living in a giant pile of litter!"

At her mention of Striper, Josh glanced over at the wire cage. The hamster was still acting strange, not eating much and wanting to sleep a lot. It had been almost a week since he had done one of his favorite tricks— climbing to the top of his wire cage to hang upside down like a fat, furry bat.

"How's he doing, anyway?" Mrs. Dennis asked.

Josh walked over and pressed his face close to the cage. Striper was sprawled on his side on top of the litter, panting furiously. "How ya' feeling, boy?" he asked. Striper didn't even look at him.

Mrs. Dennis had followed him over to the cage. "Poor little thing," she murmured. She opened the cage and carefully drew Striper out on her palm, stroking him with one finger. "See if you can at least get him to drink something, okay?"

"Okay." Josh took Striper and rubbed him against his cheek. "You're going to be okay, Stripe. Don't you worry."

After school the next day, Josh raced straight home. "Mom?" he called, tossing his backpack on the couch.

"In here." Josh followed her voice into the laundry room. "Striper's still hanging on," she said, seeing his face. "I've been checking on him all day." She gave him a funny look. "But—well, honey, I think there's something I need to talk to you about."

"What?"

She slammed the lid of the washer and cranked the knob around. When the sound of rushing water filled the small room, she walked back into the kitchen, closing the door behind her.

"Okay, here's the story," she said. "Kirk's mom dropped by this morning, and I took her back to your room to look at Striper. We took him out of his cage for a minute."

"What happened?" Josh asked, alarmed. "Did you drop him or something?"

"No, nothing like that. It's just that she told me something about Striper that really surprised me." Mrs. Dennis hesitated, but then plunged on: "Um, I guess the best way to say it is that Striper turned out to be more like a 'Stripette.'"

Josh's eyes grew wide. "You mean Striper is a girl?"

"Yep. But in hamster years, she's more like a little old lady. That's why she's been so droopy lately."

Josh thought about that for a moment. "Is she dying of old age or something?"

Mrs. Dennis said, "Well, I don't really know about that. Let's just hope for the best."

Josh was silent for a moment. "I'm going to go see him—I mean her," he said. "I still love him, even if he's a girl."

That week passed quickly. Striper stayed about the same. As Friday approached, the day the Boy Scout troop would be leaving for the campout, Josh and Terry Nelson got more and more excited.

"We're going to see an old mine called the 'Hidden Treasure,'" Josh said as they lounged on the grass in his front yard Thursday afternoon. "Maybe while we're exploring we'll find where it's hidden, right?"

Terry laughed. "Sure, Josh. I bet they're not even going to let us go inside."

"Yes, they are," Josh insisted. "I heard my dad talking to the Scoutmaster about it. A bunch of the older Scouts have already been to the mine a couple of times. Mr. Weaver told Dad they're going to take us inside in groups. And he said there's an old ghost town somewhere right around there, so maybe we'll get to explore that, too."

Terry grinned. "Maybe instead of treasure we'll find ghosts down in the mine. You know, in the *dark*. Oo-ooo!" They both laughed.

On Friday, Josh hurried straight home from school and rushed into the house—then stopped, his nose wrinkling at the smell of fresh paint.

"Josh, don't touch any of the walls!" his mother yelled from somewhere. The furniture was all draped with cloths. Josh shook his head, glad he and his dad would be leaving soon.

Mr. Dennis came home early to pack for the trip. "Hey, son, how's it going?" he asked. "About ready to head out for the mountains?"

"Sure am. I'm just glad Terry's going along so I'll have someone to talk to. The older kids always ignore me."

"Yeah, well, I think you'll have a good time." Mr. Dennis glanced at the pile of camping equipment on the counter. "Why don't you wash all our camping dishes before I pack them? Then go grab your mom's sleeping bag and an extra pillow."

"Okay. And I want to find my pocketknife before we go."

After finishing the dishes, Josh ran over to the Nelsons' to help Terry pack. A few minutes later the two boys staggered through the front door, arms piled high.

"Where do we put all this stuff?" Josh asked his dad, peeking up over the clothes and blankets in his arms. He had Terry's flashlight pinned under his chin to keep it from rolling off the top. Terry was right behind him.

"Take it outside and dump it in a pile on the front lawn. Everybody's meeting at the Weavers' before heading out. We'll carry it all over there in a few minutes."

"We're gonna *walk?*" Josh asked in disbelief. "With all this stuff?"

"It's just around the corner. Your mother's using the car to take your brother and sisters over to Grandma's. Besides," Mr. Dennis added, eyes twinkling, "it shouldn't be any problem for two rough, tough Boy Scouts— right?" His dad grinned, but Josh rolled his eyes.

A few minutes later Mrs. Dennis came out of the house balancing Jake on one hip, Danielle and Terra bouncing along behind her. She walked over to her husband and kissed him on the cheek.

"We're going to Grandma Budd's now," she said. "You guys have a good time on your campout, okay? And be careful." She leaned down to kiss Josh and ruffle Terry Nelson's dark hair. "See you tomorrow night."

After she left, Josh, Terry, and Mr. Dennis checked one more time to make sure they had everything.

"Sleeping bags?" Mr. Dennis asked, reading the packing list. "Tents? Flashlights? Canteens?"

Josh and Terry dug through the mound like two khaki-clad moles, nodding as they located each item. Finally, Mr. Dennis loaded the boys down with camping gear and filled his own arms as well.

"Time to move out!" he announced.

They marched down the sidewalk toward the Scoutmaster's house, laughing at how stupid they must look to the neighbors. They were almost there when Josh remembered his pocketknife.

"I know I was using it a couple of weeks ago, but I haven't seen it since then. I looked everywhere!"

"Well, it really doesn't matter," Mr. Dennis said. "It's not like you'll have to survive alone in the wilderness or anything. We'll have all the comforts of home—tents, sleeping bags, even 'gourmet' meals cooked over a campfire! Who could ask for anything more?"

Josh laughed. "Yeah, right, Dad."

On the Road

"Gross, Adam! Put it back in your mouth!" The chorus of boyish groans from the back of the yellow van was too loud for the two adults in the front to ignore.

"Adam!" said Ron Van Sleeuwen, Adam's father, who was driving. "Don't be a troublemaker!" Mr. Dennis, in the passenger seat, just smiled and shook his head.

Sitting in the farthest back seat, Adam grinned and popped a bloated, neon-green wad of gum back into his mouth. "There, happy now?" he asked the other boys around him. Except for Josh, they all laughed.

"Hey, Josh, you okay?" Adam asked, noticing for the first time how quiet his friend had been for the last thirty minutes, ever since the road had turned bumpy. "You want a piece of my candy or anything?"

Josh groaned. "No, thanks. I don't feel very good." At the last gas station, when most of the boys had loaded up on candy, he had stayed in the van. Now he clutched his stomach and leaned sideways against the window, trying to get more comfortable. His face looked a little green.

"Mr. Dennis!" Adam called. "I think Josh is carsick!"

Mr. Dennis looked back. "Why don't you guys make some room for him to lie down? Maybe he can sleep the rest of the way." Adam and Terry scooted over, and Josh gratefully curled into a ball on the seat. He didn't wake up until the van lurched to a stop about thirty minutes later.

He sat up dazedly, noticing that they had pulled off the side of the road. Towering all around them were the Oquirrh Mountains, rugged slopes broken with craggy rock outcroppings and thick stretches of forest. Behind them, the rest of the cars carrying Troop 845 had also stopped.

"Where are we?" he asked groggily as some of the other boys jumped out of the van. "Are we already at the mine?"

"We've still got a couple of miles to go," Mr. Dennis explained. "We just stopped so some of the boys can earn their camping merit badges by hiking the rest of the way."

Josh perked up. "Can I go with them? I'd rather walk than ride any more."

Mr. Dennis shrugged. "I guess so. Are you sure you feel up to it?"

"I'm okay. Besides, Terry and Adam are both going. We can stick together."

The boys who got out waited until all the cars and vans passed them going up the steep, winding road and then started up after them. It was hard walking, and several of the older Scouts were soon out of breath. Josh, thin and wiry, had no trouble keeping up with the group.

As they got closer to the level area marking the entrance to the Hidden Treasure Mine, they started noticing old mine shafts dotting the surrounding slopes. Some were dug sideways into the hillside; others went straight down. In the canyon below, they spotted what was left of the once-booming mining town of Jacob City.

"It must have been neat to live here when the mine was still open," said Josh. "Instead of a paycheck, I guess you'd just bring home a sack of gold each week!"

The sun was dipping low in the sky as they reached the campsite. Some of the boys who had ridden the rest of the way were already setting up their tents while others scavenged the rocky hillside for firewood. Josh found his dad and sat down to rest for a minute.

"How was your walk?" Mr. Dennis asked. "Are you feeling any better?"

"I think so. What are we having for dinner?"

"Beef stew. I'm getting ready to start it now. Why don't you just take it easy for a while?" Josh nodded and wandered off in the direction of a group of boys.

Thirty minutes later, as the sun disappeared behind the mountains, the hillside slowly came alive with bobbing flashlights and the flickering, red-orange glow of campfires. Some of the boys were playing flashlight tag while waiting for dinner. Their laughter and shouts echoed clearly in the still night air as they tried to pinion each other in the beams of their flashlights. Josh, still a little queasy, decided just to watch.

Finally Mr. Weaver and some of the other Scout leaders shouted, "Food!" causing an instant stampede toward the camp. Josh accepted a bowl of beef stew and sat down cross-legged next to the fire to eat it.

"Mm-mm!" he said, scooping a warm mouthful of beef and boiled potatoes into his mouth. "This is great!"

Mr. Dennis smiled. "Everything always tastes better outdoors, doesn't it? I wonder why that is?"

"Probably because you're starving to death before you get it," Josh mumbled, his mouth full. Mr. Dennis laughed and nudged him playfully with his foot.

Josh was finishing up a second bowl when he noticed a group of boys gathering over by the mine entrance. He went over to find out what was happening.

"We're going inside to explore!" Adam Van Sleeuwen told him excitedly. "Mr. Weaver says it doesn't matter whether it's day or night outside, because inside the mine it's dark all the time. You want to come?"

Josh ran back to his dad. "A bunch of guys are going inside the mine. Can I go with them?"

Mr. Dennis looked doubtful. "I don't know. I need to clean up this mess from dinner. How many leaders are going?"

"A bunch of them. Mr. Weaver and Mr. Powell, I think. Terry Nelson's going in. Please, can I go?"

Mr. Dennis glanced over at the group outside the mine. Scoutmaster Kevin Weaver was standing there in front of the boys, raising his voice slightly to carry over their excited chatter.

"Each of you will need a flashlight," he was saying. "You'll have to stay together and keep your adult leader in sight at all times. There are a lot of dangerous pits in there, so you'll need to shine your light at your feet. Okay?"

There was a unanimous chorus of agreement from the boys. Mr. Weaver knelt and then lowered himself through the three-foot opening into the mine. The other boys followed one at a time. "Dad?" Josh said urgently. "Can I go please?"

Mr. Dennis sighed. "All right, all right. But listen—you pay attention to what Mr. Weaver said, you hear me? I'll be along in just a few minutes."

"Okay!" Josh said. "Thanks!"

After grabbing his dad's flashlight and a handful of licorice bits for dessert, Josh raced over to the mine entrance where the last few boys were just climbing down. He was the last one in line to lower himself through the narrow opening leading down into the cool, underground darkness of the Hidden Treasure Mine.

He was surprised when his cleats hit the dusty floor of the mine shaft with a muffled *thud*. He immediately swung his flashlight around, curious.

The other Scouts were already heading off, single-file, down the main tunnel, their wildly bobbing flashlights casting eerie shadows on the tunnel walls. Their voices also sounded oddly muffled. The air smelled musty and damp and was surprisingly chilly. Josh was glad he was wearing his blue and gray parka.

He took several quick steps in the direction of the group before remembering Mr. Weaver's warning about pits. He pointed the flashlight down at his feet as he hurried to catch up. They were following some kind of underground railroad track—probably what the old ore carts rolled along. He smiled at the picture of carts heaped with gold and silver. Maybe if he looked close enough he'd spot a chunk they'd dropped.

Hidden Treasure. What a great name for a mine!

Down into Hidden Treasure

Still lagging behind the others, Josh darted the beam of his flashlight back and forth over the floor and up the walls. They looked as if they'd been cut through solid rock. He didn't see any gold, but he did spot several interesting pieces of junk—rusted railroad spikes, chunks of rotting wood.

Stopping to examine a twisted piece of iron, he was startled, when he looked up again, to discover that the others had moved out of sight around a bend. He was surprised at how silent—and dark—the shaft had suddenly become. He quickly ran to catch up.

A few minutes later they reached an open chamber, and Mr. Weaver had everybody gather around him.

"Before we go any deeper," he said, "I want to remind you guys about how important it is to stay together. I know it's a lot of fun to fool around down here—" he looked over at a couple of boys who were shining their flashlights on their faces and grinning at each other, "but the fact is, it can be dangerous."

He paused. "Let's do something. Everybody turn off your flashlights for a minute." One by one the flashlights were clicked off amidst a ripple of laughter. Finally, the tunnel was left in total blackness. After a moment the murmur of voices also died away, leaving a heavy silence broken only by a hollow dripping sound and a few nervous whispers. In the darkness, the damp, chilly air seemed even colder.

Mr. Weaver's voice broke the silence. "Can you imagine," he said, "being stuck in here without a light? You'd never find your way out. Now you can see why it's so important to stay together." He clicked his flashlight back on, and with a sigh of relief the boys did the same.

Josh was glad when they started forward again. They peered into a few side tunnels and looked at some scribbles on the walls, but after a few minutes Josh decided to go back up the tunnel and meet his dad.

He slowly worked his way along the old rail tracks until he was almost to the entrance again. Where was his dad? He had said he was coming in just a minute.

Josh heard voices and footsteps in the tunnel ahead and then could see lights bouncing off the walls. As he watched, several shadowy figures stepped around a bend and aimed their flashlights straight at him. Squinting into the glare, he called out, "Dad, is that you?"

"Josh?" a hollow voice answered in reply. When the light moved away from his face, Josh saw four figures: Cary, Tyler, and Danny, all older Scouts, and his dad. Mr. Dennis didn't have a flashlight, since Josh had taken his.

"Hi, son!" Mr. Dennis greeted him with a smile. "You coming or going?"

"Neither. I just came back to wait for you."

"Where's everybody else?"

Josh pointed. "They're all back there."

"Great! Let's get going and see if we can catch up with them." He paused. "Josh, can I hold your flashlight for Danny? His batteries are dead, and I don't have one."

Danny, a visually impaired Scout, wasn't finding the experience of shuffling over uneven ground in a dark tunnel a pleasant one. "Sure," Josh said, handing over the flashlight. Mr. Dennis held it up as they started forward again.

Soon they spotted the flickering lights of the first group in the tunnel just ahead. Danny, however, was still having a hard time seeing.

"Mr. Dennis, can I please go back?" he asked. "This really isn't much fun for me. Everything's just a big blur."

"No problem," Mr. Dennis said. "Just hang on a minute and let me tell the others."

Josh was a few steps ahead, with Cary and Tyler; in front of them the large group was in clear sight. "Hey, guys!" Mr. Dennis shouted. "I'm taking Danny back out, so you need to hurry and catch up with the others. Josh, you want to come with us?"

Josh paused and looked back. "Do I have to?"

Mr. Dennis shrugged. "No, I don't guess so. But I'll need your flashlight to get Danny back out of here."

"That's okay. Cary and Tyler both have lights."

Mr. Dennis nodded and then turned to lead Danny back the way they'd come. Josh turned in the other direction to go with Cary and Tyler. He was surprised to see how far ahead their bobbing lights had gotten.

"Hey!" he exclaimed. He started after them, but without his flashlight he couldn't go very fast. He'd only taken a few steps in their direction when their lights totally disappeared. He stopped, unable to see.

Guess I'll have to go with Dad and Danny after all, he thought. But when he turned around, there was nothing but darkness in that direction, too.

He frowned and then yelled, "Dad?"

He held his breath and listened, hoping to hear faint voices or footsteps, but all he heard was a distant dripping sound. He stood for a moment in indecision, feeling the eerie blackness closing in around him like some kind of clammy blanket.

It was just like when Mr. Weaver made them all turn out their flashlights—only this time, it was for real.

* * *

"Wasn't that neat when we all turned out our flashlights? It was like being on another planet."

"Feels warmer out here. I was freezing in there!"

Mr. Dennis smiled as, one by one, the boys popped back up out of the mine entrance, chattering and laughing. Some made a beeline to the campfire to get a second helping of stew while others scampered up the rocky hillside for another round of flashlight tag. Mr. Dennis kept glancing over at the entrance, watching for Josh.

He wasn't concerned until Mr. Weaver and his group climbed up out of the shaft. Josh wasn't with them.

"Kevin!" Mr. Dennis called to the Scoutmaster. "How many boys are still down there?"

"Not many. Rick's with some of the older boys scouting around that one dead-end shaft, but that's about it."

"I guess Josh went with them?" he asked.

"Josh? I don't think so. Didn't he come out with you?"

"No, he went with Cary and Tyler to join your group."

Mr. Weaver started to say something but stopped. "He might've come out with one of the other groups," he said, glancing at all the Scouts milling around. "It's hard to keep track of them as fast as they move. Let's ask around to see if anybody's seen him."

Several younger Scouts had been sitting near the mine entrance. "Did any of you see Joshua Dennis come out?" asked Mr. Weaver. "His dad is looking for him."

The boys shook their heads. Mr. Weaver turned back to Mr. Dennis. "I'll bet he's running around out here somewhere. Let's go find Cary and Tyler; maybe he's still with them."

When they found the two older Scouts, though, they shook their heads in bewilderment.

"He didn't go with us," Cary told Mr. Dennis. "Remember? We met him when we were first going in, but then he went back out with you and Danny."

"No, he didn't," Mr. Dennis's voice sounded strained. "I asked him if he wanted to, and he said no. I sent him back with you guys."

Cary and Tyler looked at each other. "We never saw him after that," Tyler said. "We were going pretty fast, trying to catch up with Mr. Weaver's group. Maybe Josh couldn't keep up. Still," he added, "he shouldn't have had any trouble finding us as long as he stayed in the main tunnel. Even though it twists around a lot it's not really that complicated."

Mr. Dennis's face was suddenly grim. "I took his flashlight. Well, *my* flashlight, but I had to take it. Danny's was dead. Josh didn't have another one with him."

His words brought a shocked silence to the small group.

"Well, let's have another quick look around out here before we jump to any conclusions," Mr. Weaver said. "You boys go check the tents; Josh was feeling sick earlier, so maybe he just crawled into a sleeping bag and dozed off. Terry and I will scout around and see if he's off playing tag or something."

He turned back to Mr. Dennis and placed a hand on his shoulder. "I'm sure he's fine. But if he's not out here, we'll get together a search crew to go in the mine and find him. Okay?"

"Okay," Mr. Dennis said carefully. He pushed away the thought of Josh alone in the inky blackness, wandering blindly near mine shafts and other dangers. *Please, God,* he prayed. *Don't let anything happen to my son.*

* * *

Getting no answer from his father, Josh stood frozen in the misty darkness, his heart pounding. What should he do?

"Dad!" he screamed again. His voice sounded strange, like it was being swallowed up by the darkness. "Dad, come back!" After a moment, though, he calmed down. He couldn't be far from the mine entrance; he could find his way back by following the rail tracks. All he had to do was figure out which way was out.

It was weird, he thought as he groped in the direction where he thought the wall should be, how really dark it was. It wasn't like the darkness outside where you could see shadowy shapes or reflections or like closing your eyes in a bright room and you could still sort of sense light. This must be what it was like to be blind. He didn't blame Danny for not wanting to hang around down here.

After fumbling around, his hand touched cold rock. "Found it!" he exclaimed. "Now, which way should I go?"

Placing both hands on the wall, he closed his eyes and tried to picture the tunnel where he'd stopped. It was confusing, but left felt more "right" to him. He decided to go that way.

He started off slowly, trailing his right hand along the rough wall while extending his other hand out in front of him to keep from running into anything. He shuffled his feet on the dusty floor, remembering what Mr. Weaver had said about deep pits. He'd feel pretty stupid falling down in some hole!

He walked for several minutes in what seemed like a straight line, stopping every now and then to grope his way over to the rail tracks to make sure he was still following them. Several times he splashed without warning into puddles, yelping as the icy water soaked his socks and cleats. He paused to zip up his parka before continuing on.

Soon he realized that the tunnel seemed to be angling slightly upward—and that a faint, cool breeze was stirring. *I must be getting near the entrance!* he thought. *This must be that downslope we were on when we first came in.*

But after going a little farther he began to wonder. Shouldn't he have reached the entrance by now? He couldn't have missed it; he'd been peering up through the darkness every few steps, watching for the three-foot opening. Besides, the slope was much steeper now than he remembered it coming in.

It probably just seems steeper because I'm going up instead of down, he told himself. *I'll see the entrance any second.*

But the uneven slope finally grew so steep that he had to used his hands. When he slipped on the gravel, he slid backwards.

"Ow!" Josh exclaimed, rubbing his scraped knee. He sank down on the cold floor, disgusted. His hands were muddy, his jeans wet halfway up to his knee, and he was shivering. He was getting hungry again, and thought longingly of the warm campfire and leftover stew waiting just outside—if he just knew where "outside" was!

After a minute he sighed and stood up again, but he'd only taken a few steps when he banged his head, hard, on something in the darkness. He reached up to find that the tunnel ceiling was much lower than it should have been. Groping his way over toward the opposite wall, he felt for the rail tracks. They weren't there anymore. He slowly sank back down onto the floor, hugging his knees for warmth.

He had taken a wrong turn in the dark. He was lost.

The Search Begins

Outside the mine, Mr. Dennis anxiously paced back and forth. He'd already checked the tents and asked dozens of boys, including Terry Nelson, if they'd seen Josh since they'd come back out of the mine. None of them had.

"He's still in there," Mr. Dennis told Mr. Weaver. His voice broke, and he swallowed hard. "I'm going in to find him."

"I'll go with you," Mr. Weaver said. "But look, Josh might still turn up out here somewhere. I've sent a group of the boys to recheck all the tents and look in all the cars. Everybody knows now that he's missing. It's not time yet to panic."

A moment later, flashlights in hand, Mr. Dennis and the Scoutmaster dropped back down through the opening into the mine. Swinging the lights back and forth, they started down the main tunnel, shouting "Jo-o-sh!"

* * *

Josh spent another ten or fifteen minutes walking and crawling in circles trying to figure where he was, but finally gave up. He sat huddled and shivering, leaning against the cold rock wall, wondering what to do next.

Should he backtrack? He thought about that, imagining the dark journey back down the winding tunnel with no landmarks to guide him. What if he took another wrong turn? He'd be in even worse trouble.

Then he remembered something he should have thought of earlier. Every time his family went camping or to amusement parks, his mom always said, "If you get separated, just stay put. Don't move around, or it'll be that much harder for us to find you."

Guess I should've just sat down and waited when Dad went off, he thought belatedly. Now, however, he decided to take his mom's advice. He'd "stay put" and wait for his dad to find him.

* * *

"Did Josh ever turn up out here?"

The anxiety in Mr. Dennis's voice was apparent. He and the Scoutmaster had just wriggled their way back up out of the mine shaft entrance and were glancing around at the crowd of boys.

Mr. Van Sleeuwen shook his head. "Afraid not. And I think we've done a pretty good search of the area. You didn't see any sign of him in there?"

"No, none at all," said Mr. Dennis. "We went all the way back down the main tunnel and shouted into most of the side tunnels." His voice was unsteady. "If Josh fell into one of those shafts, I'll never forgive myself. This is all my fault."

Mr. Van Sleeuwen put a hand on his shoulder. "Take it easy, Terry. Let's get a search party and go through the mine. He's got to be there somewhere. We'll find him."

Within minutes, eight Scout leaders were gathered, flashlights in hand, at the entrance. Darryl Thomas, an experienced spelunker, or cave explorer, had his rappelling gear along in case they needed to climb down any of the vertical shafts.

"Okay, listen up!" Mr. Weaver said. "Let's work in small teams and check out every single tunnel we were in today. These tunnels muffle sound, so you're going to have to yell loud. We'll all meet back at the dead end of the main tunnel."

One by one, the men dropped down through the hole and fanned out. Mr. Dennis and Mr. Weaver started down the main tunnel together, following the same path they'd taken a few hours earlier.

"Jo-o-sh!" Mr. Dennis shouted. "Joshua! Can you hear me?" "Joshua Dennis!" Mr. Weaver shouted. "Yell if you can hear us!"

Their voices bounced back at them, sounding strangely hollow. But although they stopped and listened closely for a reply, the only sounds they heard were the distant echoes of the other searchers. They moved on, shining their flashlights into every tiny crack, every shadowy corner, praying that they'd see Josh.

About halfway down the main shaft they were joined by Rick Powell and Darryl Thomas. "Any luck yet?" Mr. Powell asked.

"No," Mr. Dennis said. "We went right past the spot where I turned around to take Danny out, but there's no sign of him. It doesn't make sense! He knows to just sit down and wait if he gets separated. That's what worries me the most. Something must have happened to him!"

"Don't jump to conclusions," Mr. Thomas said. "People often get lost in caves, but they usually turn up."

They continued down the mine shaft, calling Josh every few minutes. The dusty floor, criss-crossed with footprints pointing both directions, gave no clue to where one small boy might have gone. Several searchers emerged from side tunnels and joined their group.

"Look." Mr. Weaver's flashlight suddenly stopped, trained on a broken board lying on the mine floor—one of several that had been laid down to cover the opening of a deep shaft. "Was that broken when we came through here earlier?"

"I don't think so," said Mr. Powell. He walked over and knelt down to examine the board. "Looks like a fresh break." He shifted his flashlight to shine it down into the shaft. "It's pretty deep. I can't see the bottom."

He looked up, as all the men slowly turned to look over at Mr. Dennis. His face was hidden by the darkness, but his voice revealed his fear as he spoke.

"You think Josh fell in there?"

No one contradicted him. He pushed his way past the others to kneel by the shaft. "Josh!" he screamed. "Joshua, are you in there?" Although the men strained to hear any faint reply, the shaft remained silent.

"Look," Mr. Powell said. "Why don't I rappel down and check it out, just to make sure? Darryl brought along his gear."

A moment later, strapped into the rappelling harness, Mr. Powell began to lower himself foot by foot into the narrow shaft, supported by a rope held by the other men. Mr. Dennis waited, praying silently that his son's body wouldn't be at the bottom.

"Nothing here!" Mr. Powell's voice drifted up, muted, from the shaft. "Go ahead and pull me back up!"

Mr. Dennis let out his breath, almost dizzy with relief. The Scoutmaster walked over and said firmly, "We'll find him. He's probably safe and sound, sitting down here somewhere waiting for us."

* * *

Josh was, at that moment, doing exactly that. Chewing a piece of the licorice he'd found in his pocket, he was trying to pass the time until his dad returned. It was so cold that the candy was tough and hard, but it was better than nothing. In the chilled air his stomach was quivering, and his nose felt like ice.

Suddenly he sat up straight. Were those voices? He turned his head back and forth, trying to figure out which way the sound was coming from, but the solid rock walls made it confusing. The sounds were so faint and faraway that he couldn't make out the words, but they were definitely voices.

"Hey!" he yelled. "Hey, you guys, over here!"

He listened, but there was no answering call. "He-e-y! It's Josh Dennis! I'm over here!"

Instead of getting closer, the voices now seemed to be moving farther away. "Hey, come back!" he shouted. "You're going the wrong way!"

But soon the muffled silence of the underground tunnel was once again unbroken. Josh slumped back against the wall and gnawed off another piece of licorice, disappointed. Next time, he told himself, they'd hear him.

Next time.

* * *

"What were you guys thinking, taking a bunch of kids into an abandoned mine like that? Didn't you see the 'No Trespassing' signs?"

The sheriff's deputy sounded angry. It was just after midnight; after searching for more than three hours, Mr. Dennis and Mr. Thomas had finally driven into the nearby town of Tooele to ask for help.

"No, we didn't," Mr. Dennis said shortly. "Look, why don't you save the lectures for later? My son's in trouble, and he needs help—now!"

The deputy sighed. "Okay, okay. I'll call the sheriff and send a couple of men back up there with you to check out the situation."

Soon a police cruiser arrived with two deputies. After making a quick exploration of the major tunnels, the men reported that it seemed to be a genuine emergency.

Sheriff Don Proctor was notified. He called in the official search and rescue team.

The Search Continues

By nine o'clock Saturday morning, the peaceful hillside outside the mine was milling with dozens of searchers, police, and Boy Scouts. Earlier that morning the Salt Lake County Search and Rescue had also joined the search, but despite hours of combing the dark underground passages, no sign of Joshua Dennis had been found. The situation was growing more serious by the minute.

Mr. Dennis was, by now, frantic with worry. "I should call Janeen and let her know," he told Mr. Weaver, "but I just keep hoping Josh will turn up. It wouldn't be so bad for her if it was already all over and I could tell her he was okay."

"Well, I don't see the harm in waiting a little longer," Mr. Weaver said. "The sheriff finally got a map of the mine from the owners, and he says there are tunnels marked on there that we didn't even know about. Josh might have wandered into one of them."

Mr. Weaver didn't add what he was thinking: that the map, in some ways, made it all seem much worse. Instead of being the "simple" mine shaft they'd all imagined, the Hidden Treasure was actually a confusing maze of twisting passages that sprawled over six different levels. There were also countless vertical shafts, some over a thousand feet deep. To add to the problem, the map itself was old and faded, almost impossible to read. It would be a miracle if they could find, much less explore, all the tunnels it noted, some of them hidden by rock slides.

As news of the lost boy leaked out into the community, a crowd of volunteers began to gather, wanting in some way to help with the search. But Sheriff Proctor gave strict orders that only official rescue crews be allowed through the roadblock.

"We've got trained teams on the job," he told his deputies. "We don't need anybody else up here to get lost or hurt. Keep the sightseers out."

Late Saturday afternoon, a chemical foreman named John Skinner returned home from vacation to learn about Josh's disappearance. He immediately drove to the sheriff's department to offer his help. His grandfather had been the superintendent of the Hidden Treasure years before, and he had grown up playing in and around the mine.

To his surprise he, too, was turned away.

"But I know that mine like the back of my hand!" he insisted, smoothing his mustache nervously with one hand. "There are lots of places in there you'd never notice if you didn't know where to look."

"Sorry, sir. Those are the sheriff's orders."

Mr. Skinner finally gave up and went back home. *I hope they find him soon,* he thought. *With all the hidden shafts and old cases of dynamite still scattered around in there, I'd hate to be in there without a light.*

* * *

It was almost five o'clock when Mrs. Dennis pulled into the driveway, tired but triumphant. After spending hours combing the stores, she'd finally found a perfect Batman costume for Josh. She couldn't wait to see his face! She was only a little surprised to see that they weren't home yet. Certainly, they were just running a few minutes late.

She was gathering the shopping bags to carry into the house when a neighbor ran up to the car. "Janeen!" she panted. "Where have you been? We've been paging you at all the malls."

Mrs. Dennis stared at her. "Why? What's the matter?"

"It's Josh." Her voice was shaking. "The police department has been here looking for you. Terry called them a couple of hours ago. Oh Janeen, they can't find Josh!"

Mrs. Dennis froze. "What do you mean?"

"They think he's down in some mine. He went in last night and never came back out."

"He's been gone since *last night?*" Mrs. Dennis exclaimed in horror. "Oh, no!"

Now, racing toward the Hidden Treasure Mine with several close friends, she stared blindly out the passenger window. *Please, God,* she prayed. *Wherever Josh is, don't let him be scared. Send Your angels to be with him.*

* * *

Angels.

For some reason, Josh suddenly found himself thinking about them. It was a funny thing to think about, sitting all alone in the dark. He remembered his mom talked about angels a few weeks earlier during a family devotional. She didn't think they had wings and harps; she said they were messengers who helped people.

Maybe, he thought in amusement, *an angel is sitting beside me right now!*

He stretched his eyes wide, peering into the blackness. If an angel was there, he'd never know—it wouldn't even have to be invisible. He even smiled, picturing a friendly angel keeping him company in the dark. It really *felt* like somebody was there with him, and he didn't feel lonely.

He settled back sleepily, burrowing his icy hands inside his jacket for warmth. He wished he'd brought along a canteen; his mouth was getting really dry. What was taking his dad so long?

* * *

Sunday morning dawned clear and cold over the craggy slope outside the Hidden Treasure mine. The rest of the Boy Scout troop had gone home as scheduled the previous afternoon, but Mr. and Mrs. Dennis had stayed behind, waiting for word about Josh. He had now been missing for more than thirty-six hours.

A few miles away, Mr. and Mrs. Skinner were getting ready for church. Ever since the deputy had refused his help, Mr. Skinner had been trying not to worry about the boy. But he just couldn't help thinking about him, all alone in the dark like that. What a nightmare!

At church that morning, he prayed for Josh. Afterward, though, unable to stand it any longer, he drove out to the mine. He stopped at the roadblock and planted himself squarely in front of the deputy.

"I'm John Skinner," he said. "I've been in that mine hundreds of times, and I've been thinking about it. I know several places where the boy might be. I'd like to go in and check it out."

The young deputy shook his head. "I'm sorry, sir, but we've already got too many people up here as it is. We have to keep the search effort controlled. The best thing you can do is go on back home."

Mr. Skinner argued, but finally turned away in frustration. What was wrong with these people?

Monday morning passed with no sign of Josh, and by late afternoon Sheriff Proctor called his officers together.

"I think we've pretty much eliminated the mine," he said. "We've been through it from one end to the other. The boy *must* have come out and wandered off somewhere. Let's scale down the search inside and start concentrating on the mountain instead."

By mid-afternoon a massive manhunt was underway. The sheriff had set up a temporary "command post" just outside the mine from which he directed the rescue efforts.

Tracking dogs crisscrossed the rugged slopes, noses to the ground, while hundreds of searchers, including Mr.

Weaver and other friends of the family, explored every tree, rock, and bush. Three helicopters also joined the search, their rotors chopping the air overhead with a rhythmic whup-whup sound.

There was a flurry of excitement when one of the dogs sniffed out a blue Cub Scout pocketknife near a bush. But then Mr. Weaver told them that one of the younger Scouts had reported losing his knife while playing on the mountainside. The search was resumed.

Late that afternoon, Mr. Skinner decided in frustration to join the search whether the Sheriff's Department liked it or not. There was another old mine, the Buckhorn, which connected to the Hidden Treasure. He planned to sneak in through the Buckhorn and do his best to find the boy.

He drove his Ford Ranger™ around the back way, through Ophir Canyon and then hiked up the slope. It took him only a few minutes to find the Buckhorn entrance. Once inside, however, he discovered that the old tunnel connecting to the Hidden Treasure had collapsed in a pile of rotten timbers and broken rocks. Discouraged, he had to turn back. The mine was too unsafe to risk shifting things around.

He drove home slowly. The thought kept gnawing at him that if he could just get inside the mine, he might find Joshua Dennis. He remembered how the area around Resolute Stope was filled with dozens of small ore pockets that could easily be missed. If only they'd let him look!

* * *

"Mr. Dennis, can you explain why you ignored 'No Trespassing' signs to take young boys into a dangerous mine?"

"Mr. Dennis, why did you take your son's flashlight and leave him in there by himself?"

"Mr. Dennis, we've heard that Joshua argued with you right before he ran off. Is that true?"

Each time Mr. Dennis appeared at the mine site, newspaper and television reporters clustered around him to thrust microphones in his face. Many of the questions were cruel.

"They keep asking me how I could've taken Josh's flashlight like that," Mr. Dennis said later, pacing back and forth in the cramped hotel room as he talked to his wife. "And they're right! How could I have been so stupid? I *knew* better!"

"It was an accident," Mrs. Dennis said helplessly, putting her arms around him. "You're a good father, Terry, you know that. *Josh* knows that!"

* * *

Josh was sleeping fitfully on the cold, dusty floor of the mine. "Dad?" he mumbled.

The strange sound of his own voice jolted him awake. He sat up slowly, rubbing his eyes. Where was he?

It was so dark and cold. *Really* cold. The damp, frigid air burned his nose with each breath he took, and his feet and hands felt numb. He flexed his fingers and then tried to wiggle his toes. He couldn't feel his feet anymore.

Realization came back to him slowly. He was in the Hidden Treasure Mine. Without a watch to gauge time by, he had no idea how long he'd been there. Probably only a few hours, even though it seemed like forever. His mouth tasted really bad. He'd been sleeping a lot.

"Dad?" he called again in a hoarse voice. "You there?"

Nothing. Not even the faraway voices he'd heard a few times. His stomach rumbled loudly. He licked his lips, feeling how cracked and dry they were. Each time he swallowed it felt as if he had a dry lump stuck in his throat. *Heavenly Father,* he prayed, *could You please let them hurry up and find me soon? I want to get out of here.*

It was strange, but somehow the simple prayer made him feel better. He shook off his gloomy thoughts. Maybe it would cheer him up to think about some of the songs he'd been learning in school. One of his favorites was about heroes—just what he needed right now!

As he sang, the cheerful words seemed to penetrate the darkness, making him feel less lonely. Feeling around, he scooped back together the mound of soft dirt he'd been using as a pillow and then stretched back out on the floor.

Whoever gets me out of here, he told himself as he drifted off to sleep, *is going to be my hero.*

Four Days Lost

Tuesday morning, the overcast sky looked gray and threatening. After yet another sleepless night, Mr. and

Mrs. Dennis left their hotel and drove up to the mine. It was now the fourth day since Josh had disappeared. Although nobody would say it, hope was rapidly fading that he'd be found alive.

Mrs. Dennis sat watching the search efforts in a kind of daze. A specially trained mine-search crew had been called in to make a final, thorough sweep through the mine. She watched the fifteen men of the Utah Power & Light Mine Rescue team disappear into the hole one by one. They were wearing hard hats with lights and carried climbing gear and oxygen tanks. They looked efficient.

Most of the mine's honeycomb passages were decorated with brightly-colored paint or tape strips, showing that they'd already been searched. But the UP&L searchers started all over again, splitting up into three teams and spreading out to work their way down each shaft.

It was late that afternoon when they wearily gave it up for the day. But they assured Mr. and Mrs. Dennis that they'd come back the next day.

"We're not giving up hope yet, so you don't either," said Ray Guymon, the leader of the UP&L team. Mr. and Mrs. Dennis thanked them and went back to their hotel.

That night, the Dennises listened in numb silence as a TV news announcer said the official search for Josh was "winding down." Authorities were talking about sealing off the entrance to the mine as soon as the search was called off—possibly as early as the next day. If Josh was still in the cold depths of the Hidden Treasure Mine, it was almost certain that, by now, he was dead.

Mr. and Mrs. Dennis turned off the TV and tried to go to sleep, but neither of them could settle down.

"Do you think he's dead?" Mrs. Dennis finally asked.

Mr. Dennis replied, "I don't know. I keep praying for him, but I don't know anymore." He swallowed hard. "It looks like he probably is."

There was a long silence. "Do you think the sheriff would let us put up a memorial plaque for Josh at the entrance to the mine?" Mrs. Dennis asked painfully. "I mean, if they can't find his body—" her voice broke and she closed her eyes.

"We can ask." Mr. Dennis drew a shaky breath. "I'd like Kevin Weaver to speak at the funeral. Josh is—was crazy about him. I think he'd like that."

They held each other tight as they tried to decide how to say their final good-byes to their son.

* * *

A hamburger! Josh stared and then reached out with trembling hands to pick it up. It seemed like there was some reason he wasn't supposed to have a hamburger now, but he couldn't remember what it was. Anyway, he was so hungry he really didn't care. He lifted it to his lips—then realized in confusion that the juicy "hamburger" in his hand was just a cold, dusty rock.

Another dream.

The disappointment made his heart sink. He dropped the rock and sighed. He didn't feel very good, kind of weak and mixed up. Whenever he tried to think now it was as if his brain moved in slow motion. And something was wrong with his eyes; he kept "seeing" little flashes of light that weren't there. They stayed even when his eyes were closed.

He tried to wet his cracked lips, but his tongue felt like a wooden stick. His eyes were getting heavy again. He yawned and then slumped back against the rock. It was funny, but he still felt like someone was sitting right there beside him, watching over him. Funny . . .

The thought slowly faded as he dozed off again.

* * *

John Skinner stared up through the darkness at the ceiling, unable to sleep. He, too, had heard the TV news report about the mine entrance being blasted closed the next day. He was appalled. What if the boy was still inside? They'd be burying him alive!

If Josh had survived this long he would be dehydrated, and the cold air would be making his body temperature drop. He'd feel sleepy and confused. Eventually, if they didn't find him, he'd fall asleep and never wake up.

Mr. Skinner rolled over and stuffed his face into his pillow, trying to blot out the depressing thoughts. He sent up another silent prayer for the boy before drifting off into a restless sleep.

On Wednesday morning the mountain outside the Hidden Treasure was unusually quiet. Although the skies had cleared, only a handful of people still lingered at the mine site. Sheriff Proctor, exhausted and with dark circles under his eyes, remained at the nearly deserted command post. It had been a long and disheartening five days.

He nodded a weary greeting when the UP&L team showed up to search the mine one last time. He was glad that Mr. and Mrs. Dennis had decided to stay at their hotel and try to rest. They'd been through a lot.

A few miles away, Mr. Skinner was pulling on jeans and a warm wool shirt. He reflected that he felt surprisingly cheerful for having slept only a few hours. For some reason, he'd awakened that morning sure that Josh Dennis was still alive—and that he'd be found.

I'm going up there this morning, he thought. *And this time, no matter what anybody says, I'm going inside.*

On the way to the mine, he stopped for lunch. He might not get another chance at food until dinnertime. Pulling into the Penney's Service diner, he sat down at the counter, motioning to Mary Peterson, the manager.

"Hi, Mary. How about a cheeseburger and a Sprite™?"

She nodded. "Where you off to this morning?"

"I'm going up to the Hidden Treasure. I've been trying to get in there for days to look for that boy, but they wouldn't let me in. Craziest thing you've ever seen."

"I read in the paper that they're abandoning the search today. I feel so sorry for the parents." She shook her head. "What a nightmare."

"The thing is, I think I know where he might be." Mr. Skinner took his napkin and spread it open on the counter. "Can I use your pen?"

"Sure."

He quickly sketched the inside of the mine from memory, noting three places he felt Josh might be found. "See this?" he said, tapping one area with the pen. "That's Resolute Stope. There are lots of places back in there a ten-year-old could squeeze into. I bet that's where he is."

"Think he's still alive after all this time?"

"I think so. I *hope* so!"

After paying for his cheeseburger, he started toward the mine. When he reached the roadblock, he saw that the officer on duty was an old friend, so John Skinner quickly explained what he wanted to do.

The officer nodded and waved him through. "I don't see why they didn't let you in here before," he said. "You could've been a big help."

"Yeah, well, that's what I kept saying. Anyway, thanks."

Up at the mine site Mr. Skinner found Sheriff Proctor at the command post talking quietly with Ray Guymon. The UP&L team had been through every inch of the mine—twice—without finding Josh.

Mr. Skinner introduced himself. "Listen," he said, "have you guys checked the Resolute Stope area? That spot back off the main tunnel about two thousand feet in?"

Mr. Guymon looked at the sheriff, and they both raised their eyebrows. This guy seemed to know what he was talking about!

"We checked it," Mr. Guymon said. "But if you know your way around, I wouldn't mind checking it one more time. Okay with you, Sheriff?"

"Might as well. Just don't get yourself hurt."

Mr. Guymon tossed Mr. Skinner a hard hat and then motioned to another teammate, Gary Christensen, to come along. The three dropped down the hole into the mine.

Mr. Skinner quickly led the others back to one area where he thought Josh might be. They searched a small ore pocket and called Josh's name repeatedly. Nothing.

"There's another pocket right back here," Mr. Skinner said, pushing on. Again, there was no sign of Josh. Discouraged, the men paused to get a drink of water.

He's just got to be here somewhere, Mr. Skinner thought desperately. *Please, God, help us find that boy before it's too late.*

Suddenly, Mr. Guymon became alert. "What was that?"

The other two men listened, straining their ears in the darkness. Mr. Guymon was hard of hearing, so it wasn't likely that he'd heard something they'd missed.

But then they all heard it—a faint, faraway whisper of sound. They froze, afraid to even breathe.

"*Help!*"

Mr. Skinner's face split into an incredulous grin. "Josh?" he shouted. "Josh Dennis! Is that you?"

Rescued at Last!

Josh blinked slowly, his eyes sore from the dryness and dust. In the tomblike silence of the mine shaft, the only sound was his own labored breathing. What had awakened him?

Then he heard the voices. They were faint and faraway, but they were voices. With a great effort he sat up.

"Help!" he called. The sound came out like a whispered croak. He cleared his throat and tried again. "Help! Help!"

The effort left him tired and weak. He slumped back against the rock again. He was just so sleepy.

"Josh!" The voice was clearer this time.

Josh snapped back to attention, his cracked and swollen lips stretching into a smile. "Over here!" he yelled. He tried shakily to stand up, but his numb, swollen feet wouldn't support him.

"Josh!" They were getting close. "If you hear us, keep yelling so we can find you!"

A light suddenly reflected on some rocks far below. Josh squinted, dazzled by the glare. After all the hours in total darkness, it looked as bright as a spotlight.

"I'm up here!" he shouted. By the flickering light he could see the steep, gravelly slope he'd climbed, and the small ore pocket where he was sitting. He was surprised to discover that he was tucked in a cramped area surrounded by rocks. No wonder the others hadn't been able to hear him!

With a sudden burst of energy he scooted forward on his behind and started down, feet first, toward the light. He was still sliding in a shower of gravel when a sturdy-looking blond man scrambled up the slope toward him.

Reaching him, the man, Mr. Christensen, swept him up in a bear hug, and then quickly helped him the rest of the way down to where two other men—he'd later learn they were Mr. Skinner and Mr. Guymon—stepped forward, their dust-blackened faces streaked with tears.

"Boy, are we glad to see you!" Mr. Skinner said, patting his back. "Come on. We'll take you out to your mom and dad!"

"My dad is outside, but my mom's at home," Josh said in confusion. "She didn't come with us."

Mr. Skinner raised an eyebrow. "Your mom's here, too. She's been really worried." Josh didn't have the strength to argue. Why would his mom be here? He'd thought it was Saturday, but maybe he'd been in here longer than he thought. Could it already be Sunday? If so, he'd missed the whole campout!

Since his feet were too swollen to walk, Mr. Christensen carried him on his back. Mr. Skinner ran ahead to tell the others outside the good news.

Minutes later Josh, Mr. Guymon, and Mr. Christensen emerged to face a small crowd of cheering people. Sheriff Proctor had tears running down his cheeks. He gave Josh a drink of water and then had him whisked away to the hospital for a joyful reunion with his parents. Josh was astonished to learn that five days had passed since he lost his way in the darkness of the mine.

* * *

"It didn't seem that long," he said disbelievingly. "I thought it was just overnight!"

"That's good," Mrs. Dennis said, hugging him close. "We were praying that you wouldn't suffer or be lonely."

"I wasn't lonely," Josh said. "I think angels were with me. It felt like they were sitting beside me the whole time."

A few days later, pale and thin but otherwise okay, Josh was allowed to go home. When his dad turned the car onto their block, Josh was surprised to find that the neighborhood was decorated with yellow ribbons and balloons in his honor. A huge banner was draped across his street, saying, "Welcome Home, Josh!" Hundreds of friends and neighbors were standing outside, waiting to greet him.

Josh stared around him, stunned into silence. All of this was for *him?*

He was relieved to go inside the house. He hugged Jake and his two little sisters. For some reason he felt older now than when he had left. He hugged them all again, glad to be home.

Then he remembered Striper.

"Where's Striper?" he asked, suddenly afraid the cage would be empty. If Striper had died while he was gone—

"He's still hanging on," Mrs. Dennis assured him. They'd decided to keep calling the hamster a "he" since they were used to it. "But he's pretty sick. I don't think he's going to last much longer."

"I'm going to see him."

In his room, Josh lifted Striper out of the cage and rubbed him gently against his cheek. The tiny animal was barely skin and bones, too exhausted to even try to play, but he fixed Josh trustingly with his small, beady eyes. Josh felt a lump rising in his throat.

"I'm here now," he whispered. "I'm with you." He knew what it was like to need company.

Striper didn't hold out much longer. Josh wrapped the small body carefully and buried him in a box in the backyard.

A couple of days later the doorbell rang. Mrs. Dennis answered the door and saw a little boy standing beside his father. His father was holding a large wire cage.

"Is Josh here?" the boy asked shyly.

"I'll go get him," Mrs. Dennis said.

Josh came to the door. "Yeah?" he said curiously.

"My name's Brandon. I heard about what happened to you in that mine, and a friend told me about your hamster dying. I brought you something, if you want it." He added, "It's a baby guinea pig. It was born the same day you were found."

Josh bent down to look into the cage. There was a hollow log lying on top of the shredded litter, and just visible inside was a tiny, quivering ball of brown and white fur.

"He hides in that log all the time," Brandon said. "He's really cute. You can keep the cage." He looked up at his father. "My dad made it for him."

Josh turned to his mother. She was smiling. "Okay, okay," she said. "You took good care of Striper, and I'm sure you'll take good care of this one, too."

Josh nodded enthusiastically. "I've already picked a name for him." He grinned at Brandon. "Since he likes to hide in the log, I'll call him . . . Hidden Treasure!"

* * *

Some time later when Mr. and Mrs. Skinner came to visit, Josh hugged them both warmly.

"Thanks for looking for me," he told Mr. Skinner. "There was a song I kept thinking about while I was waiting. It was, 'Ev'rybody's Got to Have a Hero.' You and Mr. Guymon and Mr. Christensen were all my heroes!"

Mr. and Mrs. Dennis also hugged Mr. Skinner and then invited the couple to visit with them for a few minutes. They discussed the amazing string of "coincidences" that led to Josh being found at—literally—the last minute.

There were many questions that couldn't be answered. Why had Mr. Skinner felt compelled to come back to the mine, even though he'd been warned not to?

What made him wake up that Wednesday morning suddenly convinced that Josh was alive?

Why did the rescuers choose to stop for a drink in the exact spot where Josh could finally be heard?

How did hard-of-hearing Ray Guymon hear Josh's tiny cry for help when the others didn't?

And what about Josh's strange sense of a friendly presence in the darkness with him? And the fact that, despite going five whole days without food or water, he had come out in pretty good shape?

"The whole thing was just a miracle," Mr. Skinner said. The others quickly agreed—all except Josh.

"I wouldn't really call it a *miracle*," he said, shrugging. "I asked God to send somebody—and He did!"

Josh Dennis with his three rescuers (l-r)John Skinner, Gary Christensen, and Ray Guymon.

Do You Have a Real Kids, Real Adventures Story?

We're looking for TRUE stories for future volumes of *Real Kids, Real Adventures*—stories about real kids ages nine to seventeen who have faced danger or crisis with extraordinary courage or sometimes become real life heroes. If you have heard about such a story, we might like to use it. The first person to submit a story that we use will have his or her name mentioned in the book and will receive a free copy of that book when it is published.

* * *

Please send your story ideas to: Real Kids, Real Adventures, P.O. Box 461572, Garland, TX 75046-1572. Please include your name, address, phone number with area code, and a newspaper clipping with the name and date of the paper, and/or factual information we can use to research the story.